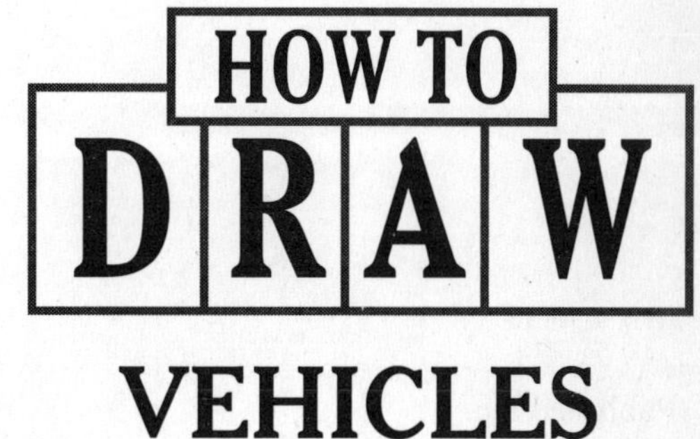

VEHICLES

PUNDALIK VAZE

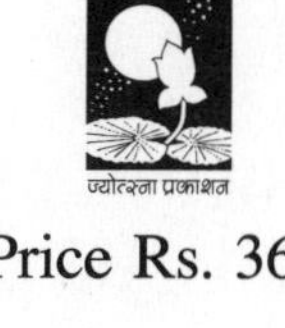

Price Rs. 36/-

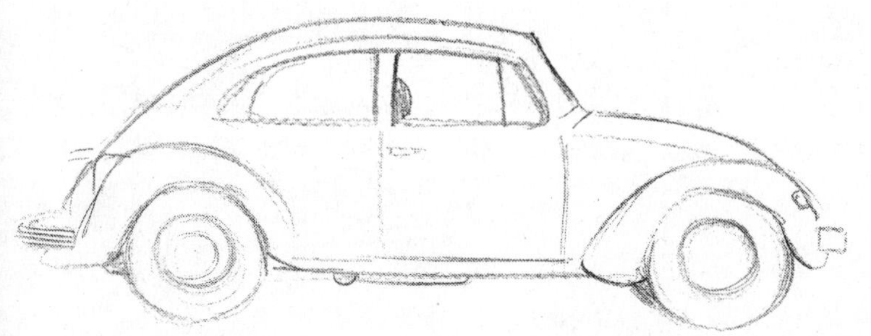

HTD VEHICLE

Published by:
Milind L. Paranjape
Jyotsna Prakashan
'Dhavalgiri'
430-31 Shaniwar Peth
Pune 411030

Mumbai Office:
Mohan Building
162 J. Shankarshet Marg
Girgaum, Mumbai 400004

First Edition:1990
Reprint: 1990, 1991, 1992
1992, 1993, 1993
1994, 1994, 1995
1997, 1998, 1999

Second Edition: 1999
Reprint: 2001, 2007, 2008,
2010

Printed by:
S. K. Printers
205 Shaniwar Peth
Pune 411030

ISBN 81-7925-001-6

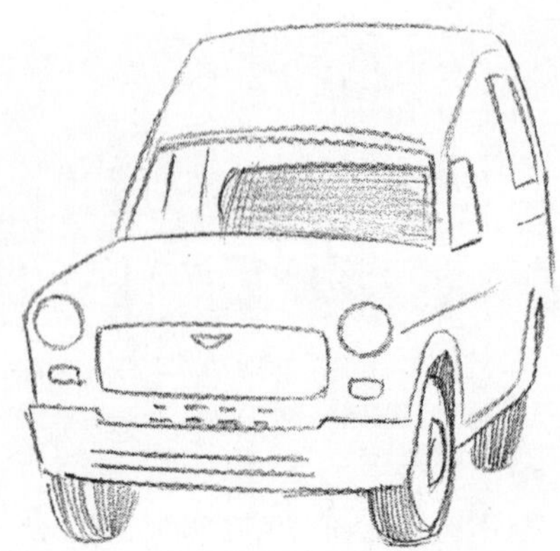

Dear little artists,

Who doesn't like fast vehicles? You young people just love them. Most of your toys are cars or other vehicles, right? And at some time or the other, you must have felt like making sketches of these vehicles, on paper.

When you begin drawing them, you do so with a lot of enthusiasm but if you can't draw them properly, you are disappointed. Let me tell you there's no reason to be disappointed.

A house is built brick by brick. Similarly, a drawing comes about step by step. In this book you will find a few simple tricks and techniques of drawing vehicles. Learn them step by step. Have a little patience and lots of practice, and you will draw vehicles fabulously.

Sachin Tendulkar has put in regular, patient and systematic efforts to reach the position of the best batsman of the world. Daily practice of many years has gone into it. The *mantra* of success is 'Practice with Patience'. If you spare and dedicate about 20 minutes to drawing every day, you will go places over the years. You can acquire mastery on lines and develop drawing skills with proper practice.

The principle of 'Perspective' plays a major role in drawing vehicles. You will know this principle as you go on reading this book. Learning it will definitely help you in improving your drawing skill not only of vehicles but of other objects as well. Soon you will realize that drawing vehicles is not as difficult as it appeared in the beginning. Also, drawing does not require a lot of instruments; a pencil and a piece of paper are sufficient.

So pick up your pencils and start right away!

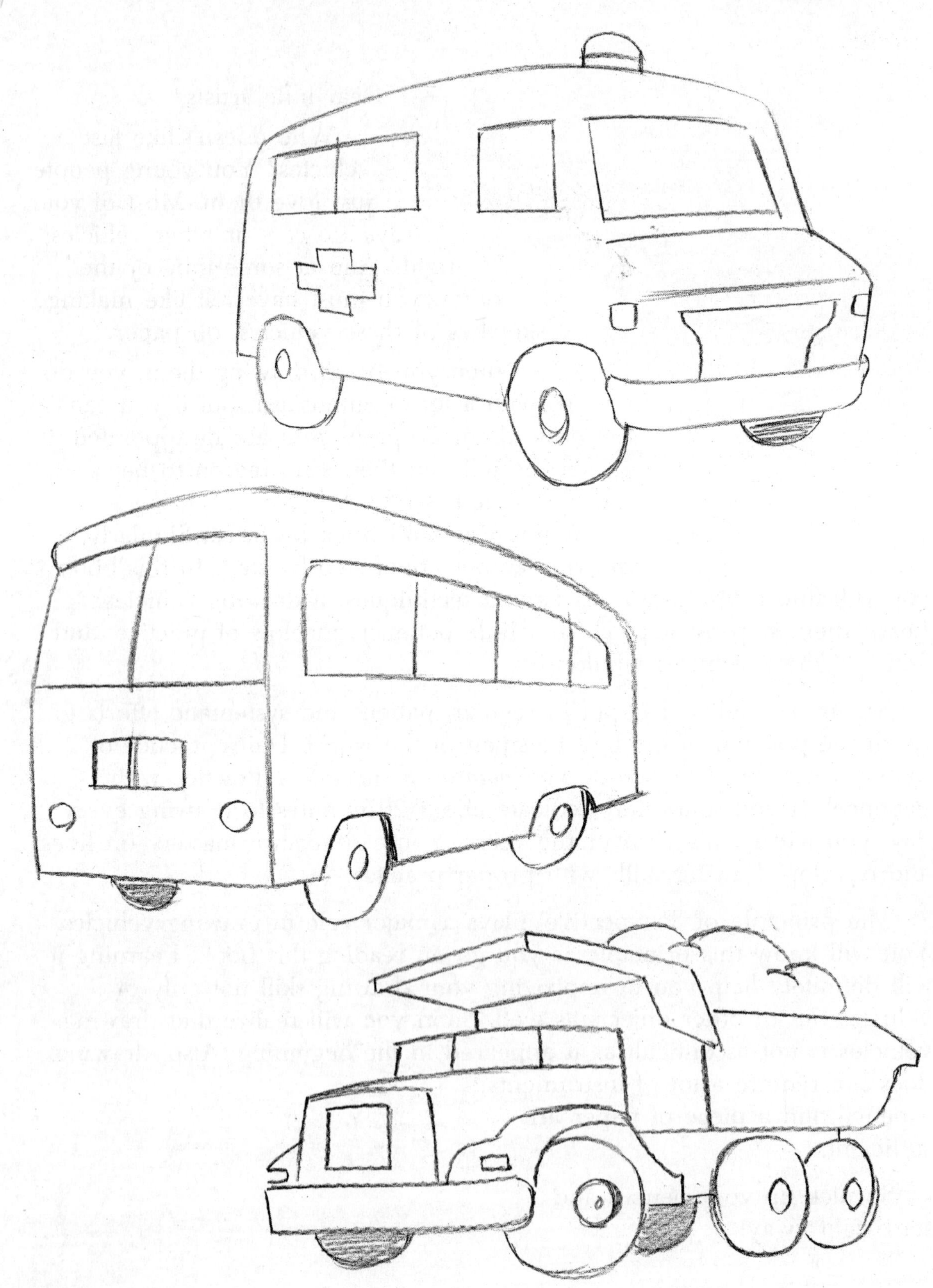

Drawing is a language of lines. With just a few lines, an artist creates an object on paper. Such is the power of lines.

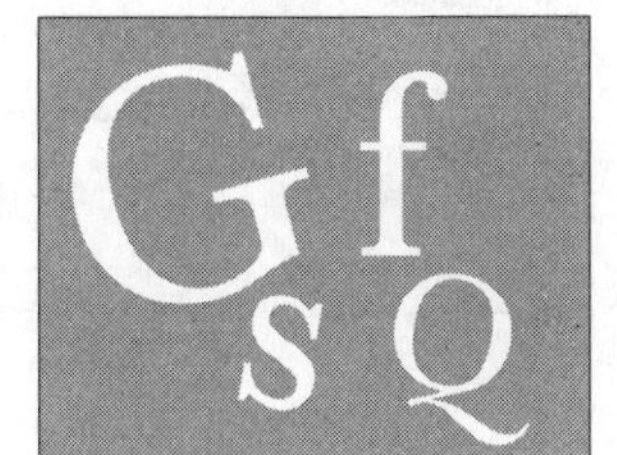

Now do not say that you cannot draw lines. What are the letters of alphabet that you write every day? They are also 'drawings' made of horizontal, vertical, straight, circular, parallel lines. And you draw them quite easily. Then what is so difficult about drawing pictures? Free and fluent drawing of these lines on a larger scale will create a picture. This can be achieved with a little practice. Once you master these lines, you can draw any picture.

Drawing vehicles is very easy. Look at the cars on the next page. These are machines and the machinery is hidden in boxes. Attach four wheels to a box and a car is ready. Of course you will have to add a few bulges, some windows and round lights to the box, but that is easy.

You do not have to be on the road to observe vehicles. You can use your toy cars for observation. Try drawing them from different angles. You may go wrong in the beginning, but ultimately you will be successful.

Keep up the practice.

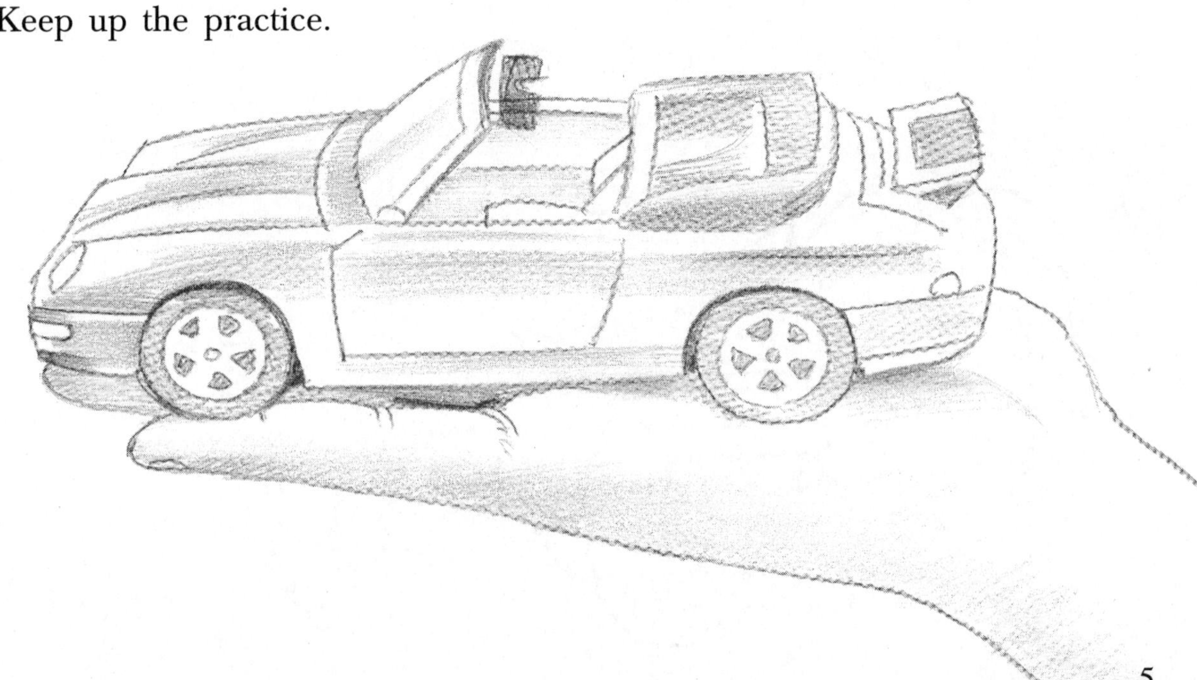

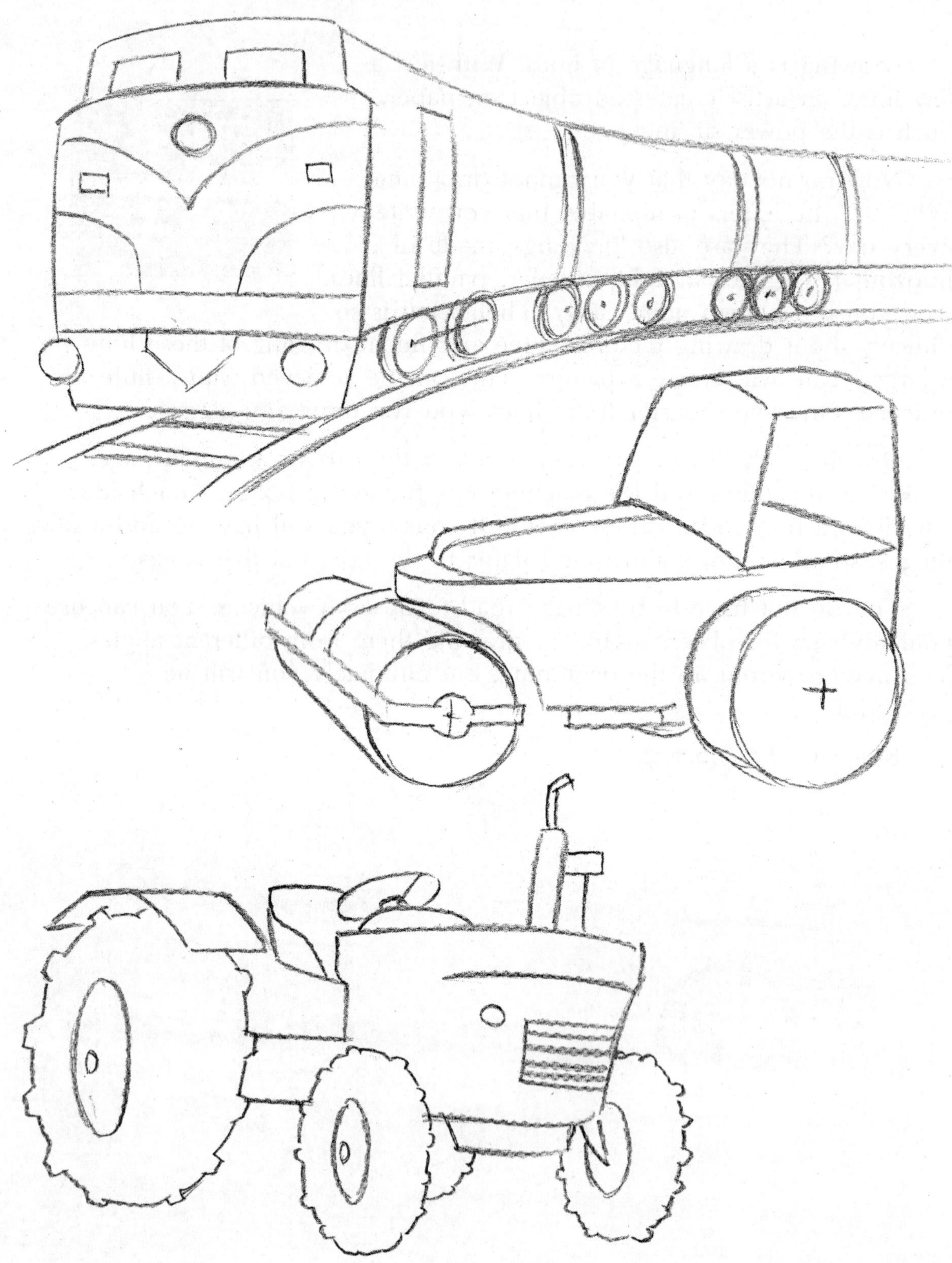

You can draw vehicles using very few lines. Practise with the pictures given here. You will easily understand how and which lines create illusions of elevations and depths.

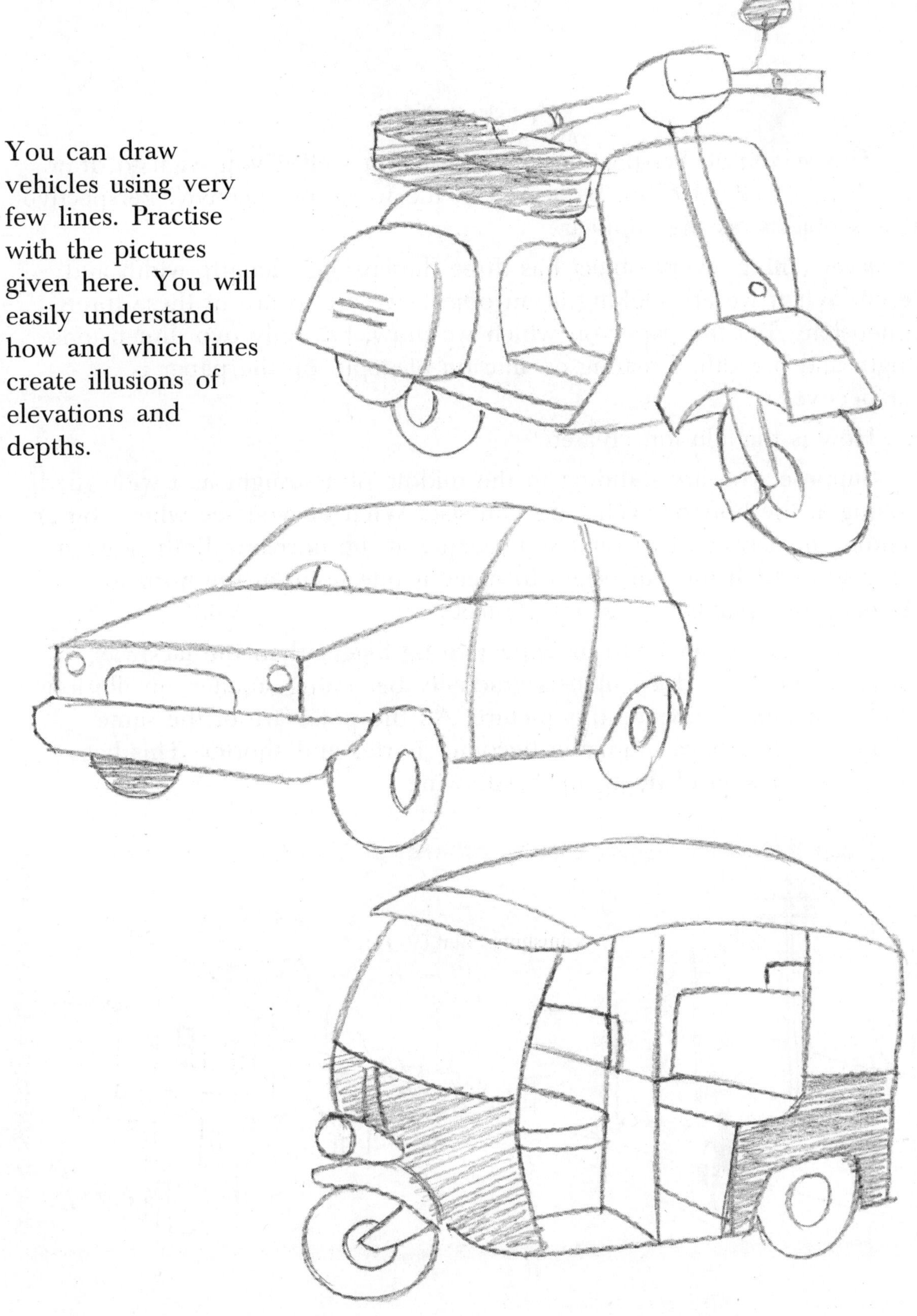

Perspective

The *mantra* of 'Perspective' must be learnt well if you want to draw vehicles perfectly. Do not be scared of the word 'perspective'. Perspective means objects 'as they appear'.

Every thing, every object has three dimensions– length, width and depth. When we are looking at an object, we are aware of these three dimensions. But the paper on which we draw, has only two dimensions– length and breadth. Creating an illusion of depth on the paper is perspective.

How is this illusion created?

Suppose, you are standing in the middle of a straight and wide road, looking at the horizon. What do you see? What do you see when you are standing in between two rails and looking at the horizon? Both sides of the road or both the rails seem to meet at one point at the horizon. (Actually two parallel lines never meet).

Also, objects nearer to us appear to be bigger than the far-away objects. When you draw objects gradually becoming smaller, an illusion of depth is created. Observe this picture. All the poles are of the same height, but they have gradually become shorter and shorter. This has created an illusion of depth in the drawing.

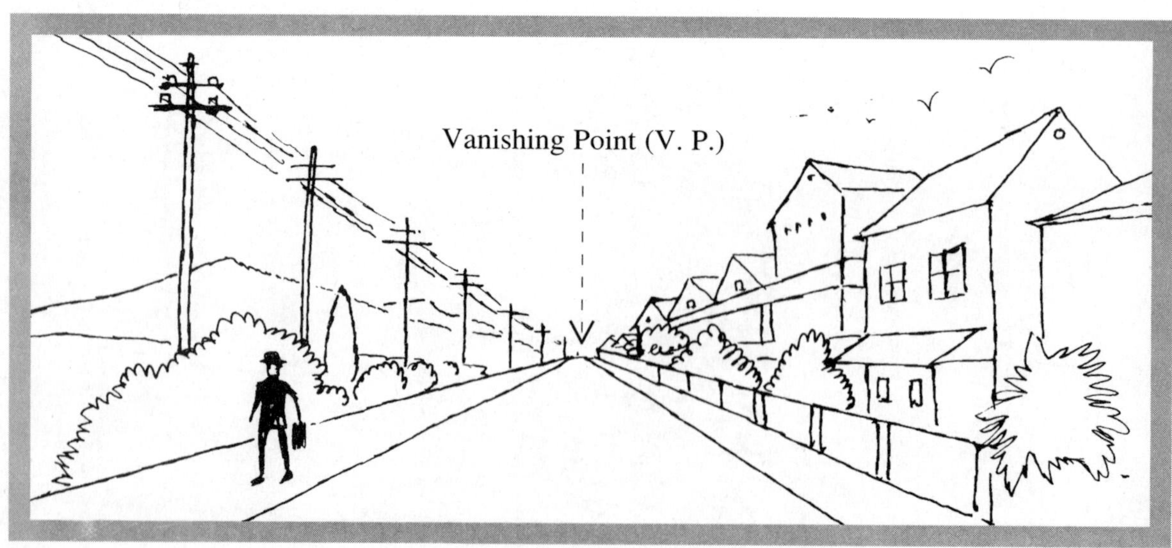

Now you know the most important principle of perspective, far-off objects look smaller than the nearer objects.

The same principle is used in this drawing of a bus. The portion close to us looks large and the farther portion looks smaller.

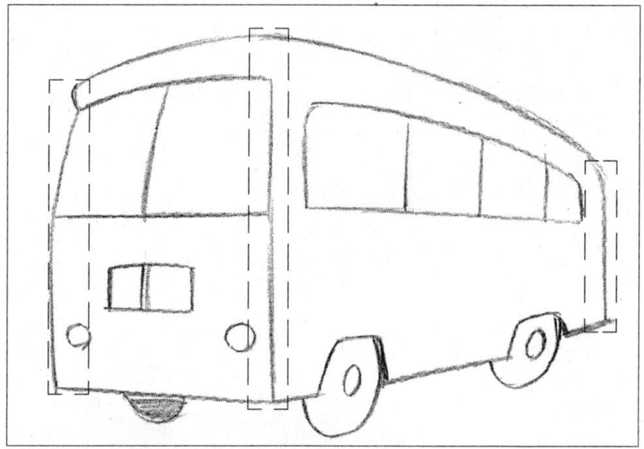

The point at the horizon (in a drawing) where all horizontal lines meet, is called the Vanishing Point.

In the drawing on the adjacent page, all the lines meet at the centre of the drawing. This type of perspective is known as 'One-Point Perspective'. Here a front view is taken.

When you look at the bus from a corner, you can see two sides of the bus. In such drawings, there are two meeting points. This is called 'Two-Point Perspective'. Drawings based on such points look perfect.

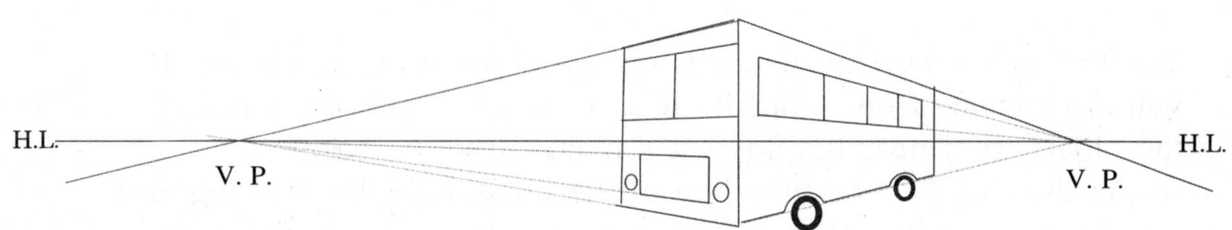

V. P.– Vanishing Point
H.L.– Horizon Line

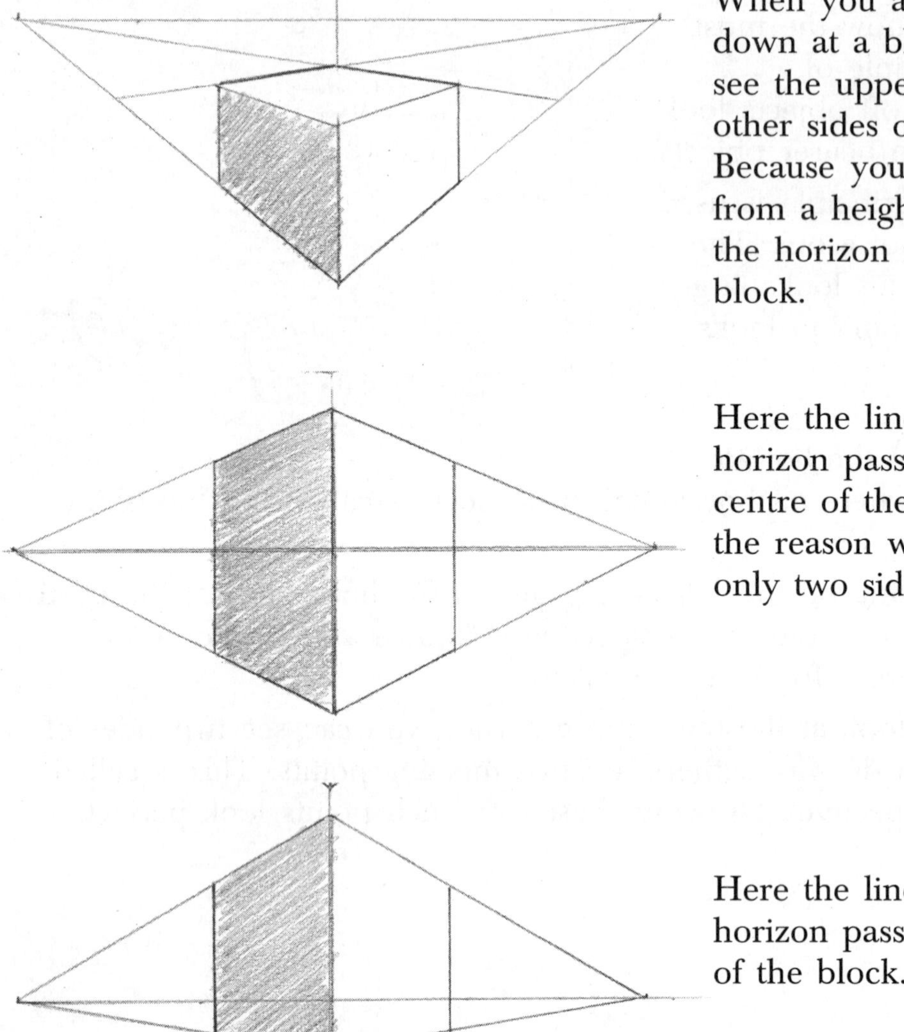

When you are looking down at a block, you can see the upper side and two other sides of the block. Because you are looking from a height, the line of the horizon is above the block.

Here the line of the horizon passes through the centre of the block. That is the reason why you see only two sides of the block.

Here the line of the horizon passes by the base of the block.

The line of the horizon depends on the position of the viewer. If you are viewing from a height, it is lifted up. If you are viewing the object from near the base, it remains near the base.
In the drawing of a car, the line of the horizon of the drawing and the vanishing points of the car depend on the position of the observer.

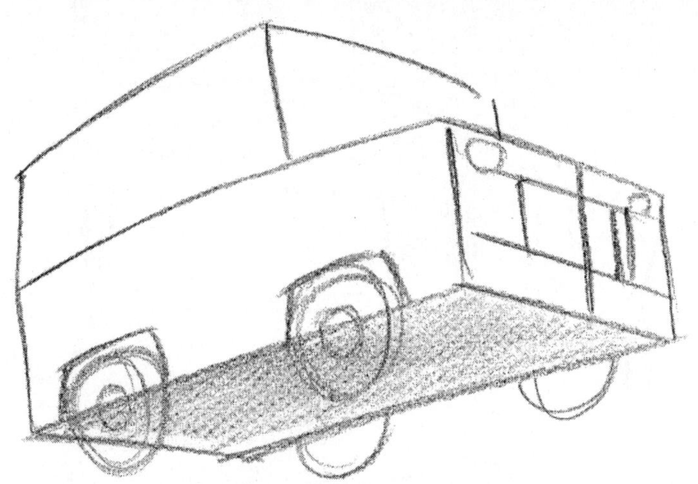

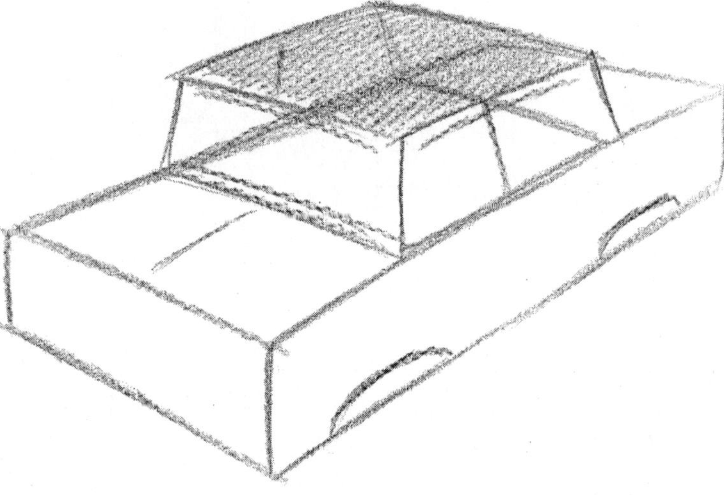

Here are some rough drawings of cars.
In the first drawing, you are looking at the car from below. In the next drawing, you arc looking at the car from above. First make such rough drawings, then think and decide the line of the horizon and vanishing points. This way, your drawings will be flawless.

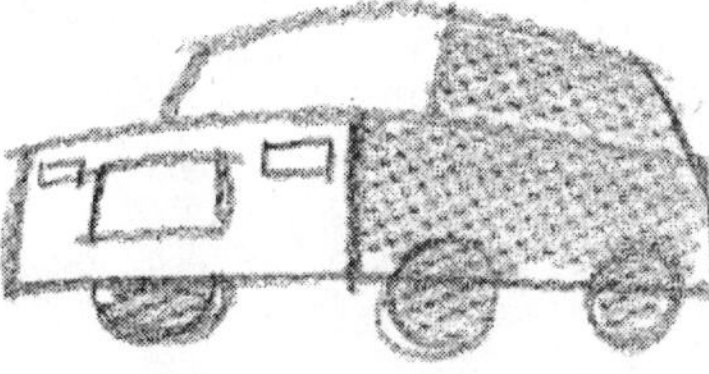

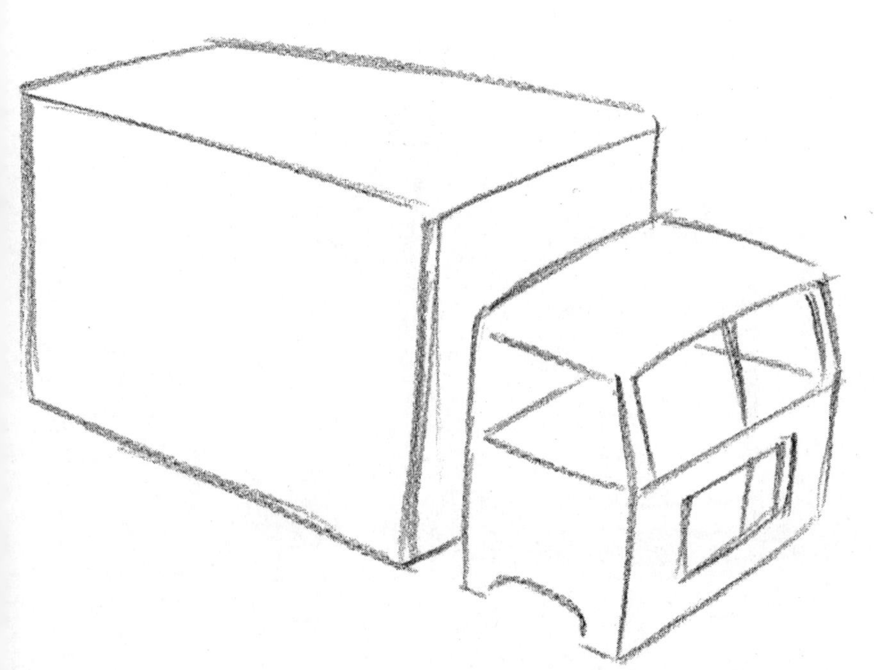

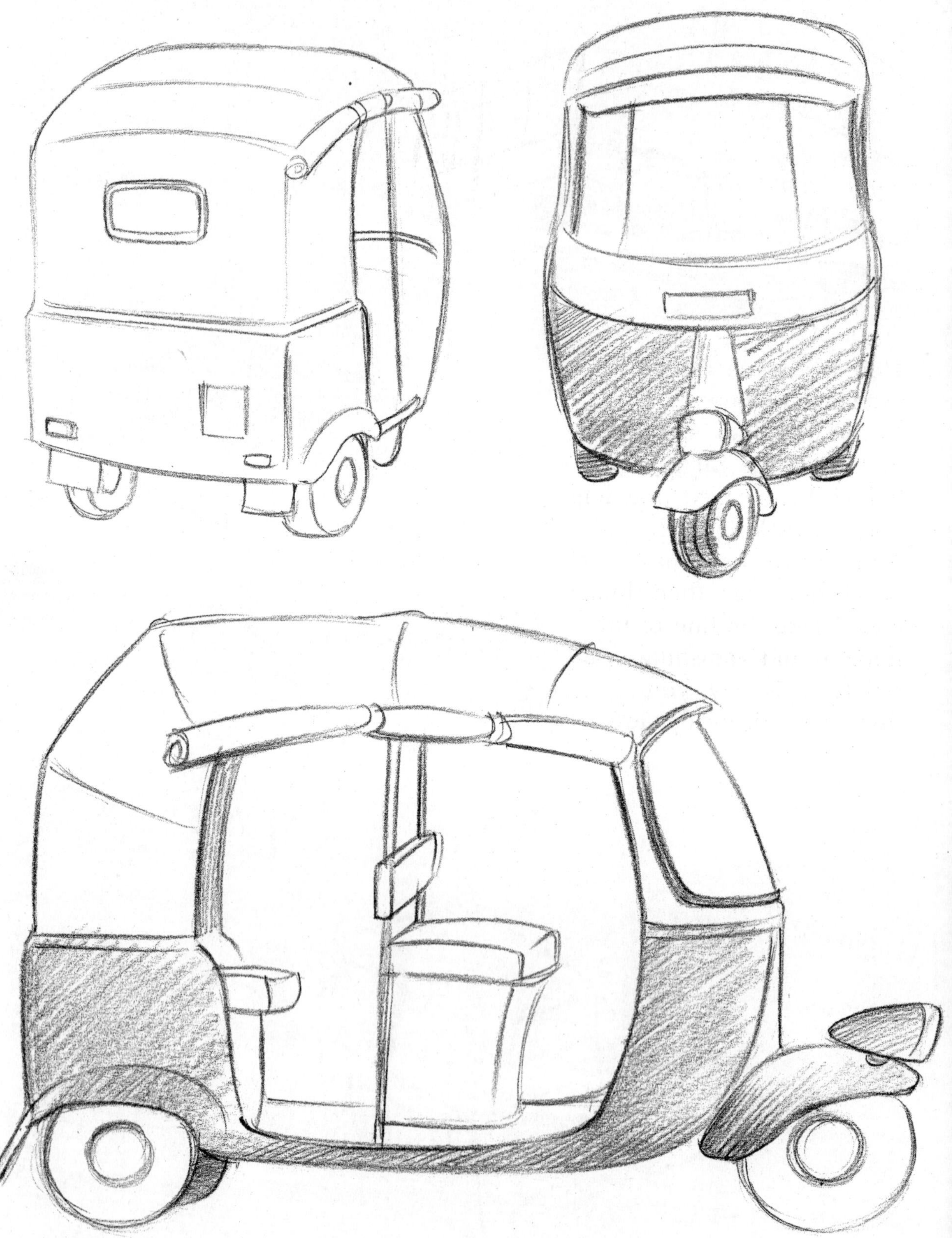

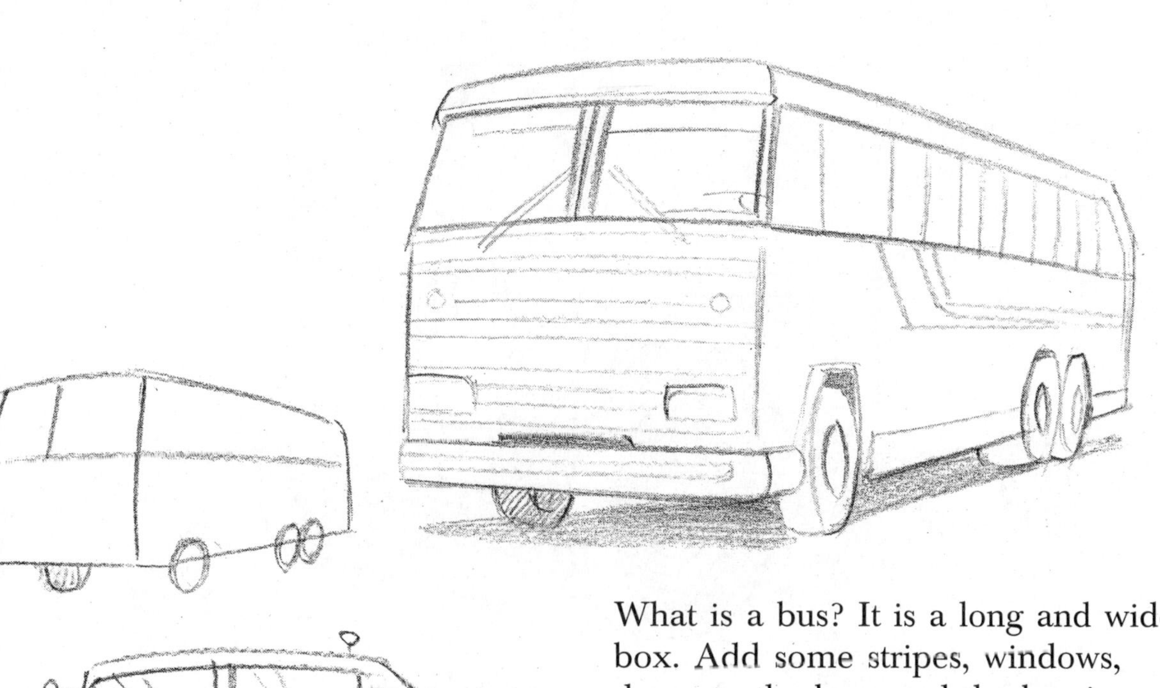

What is a bus? It is a long and wide box. Add some stripes, windows, doors to the box, and the bus is ready. You should not begin with the stripes etc. The name-plate should be the last to be drawn. First decide on the length, width, height of the body and the wheels and their positions. All these must be proportionate. Make rough drawings, then add details.

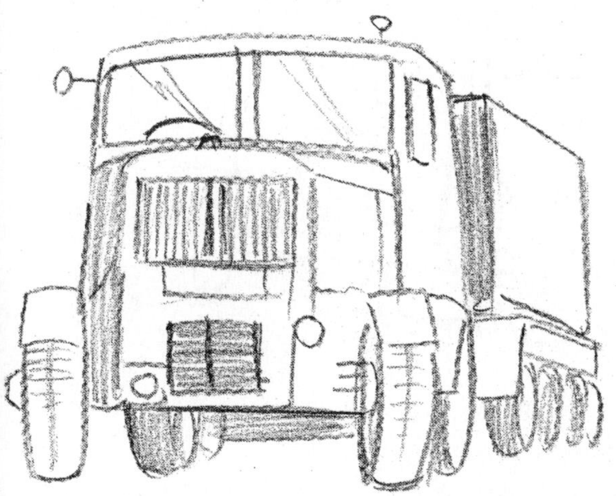

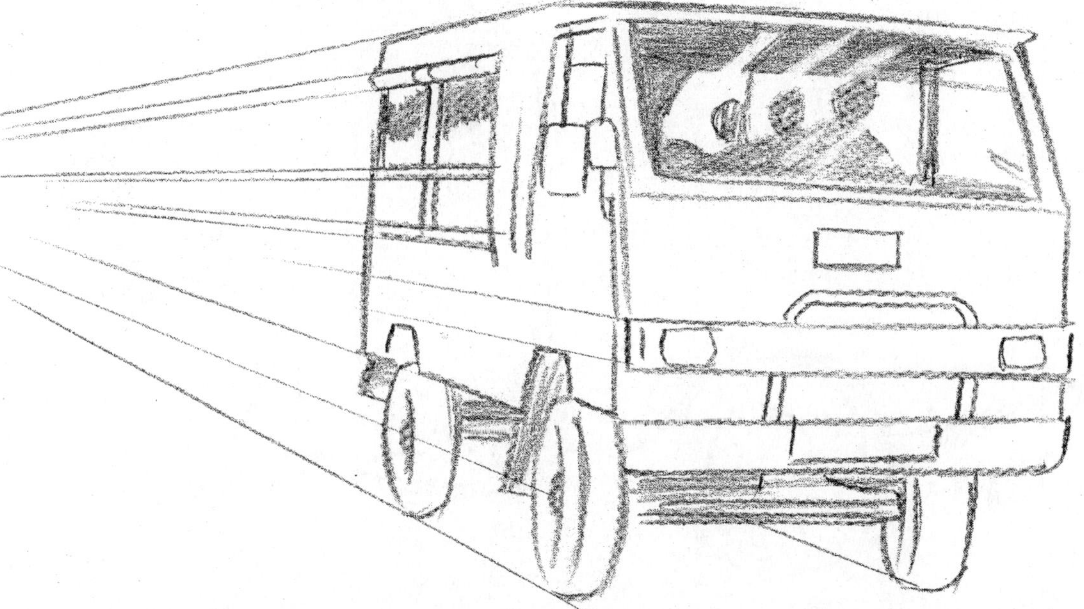

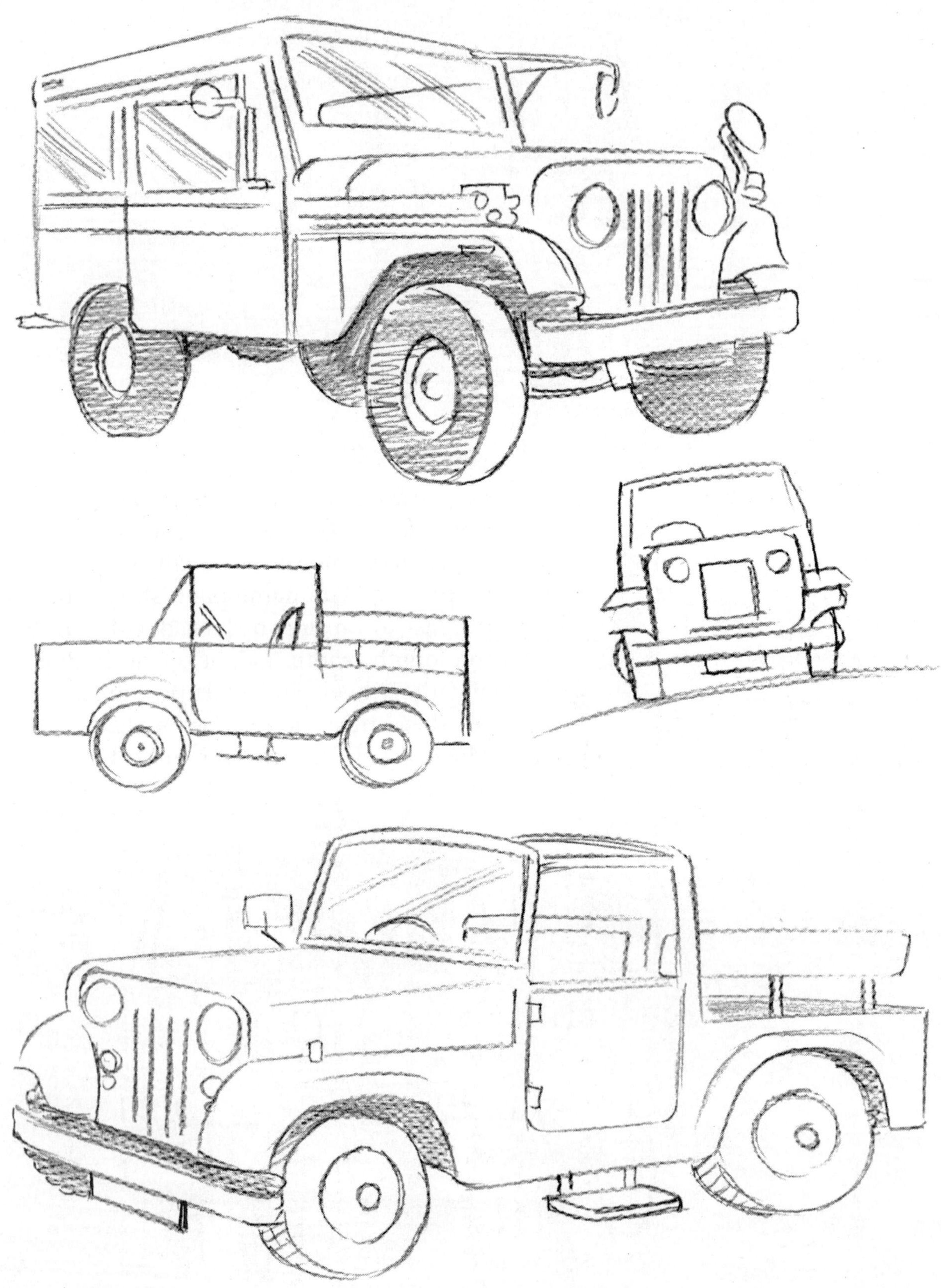

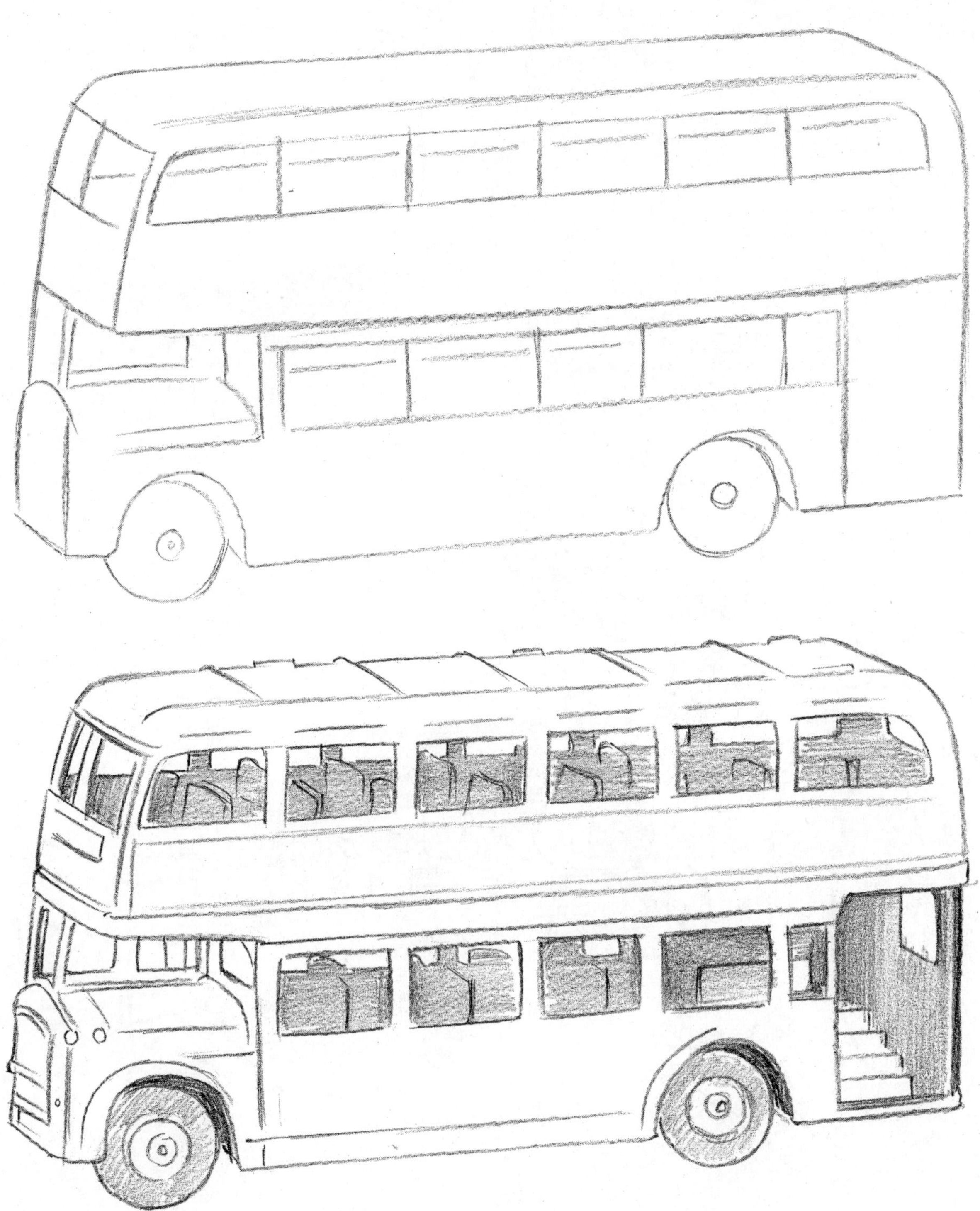

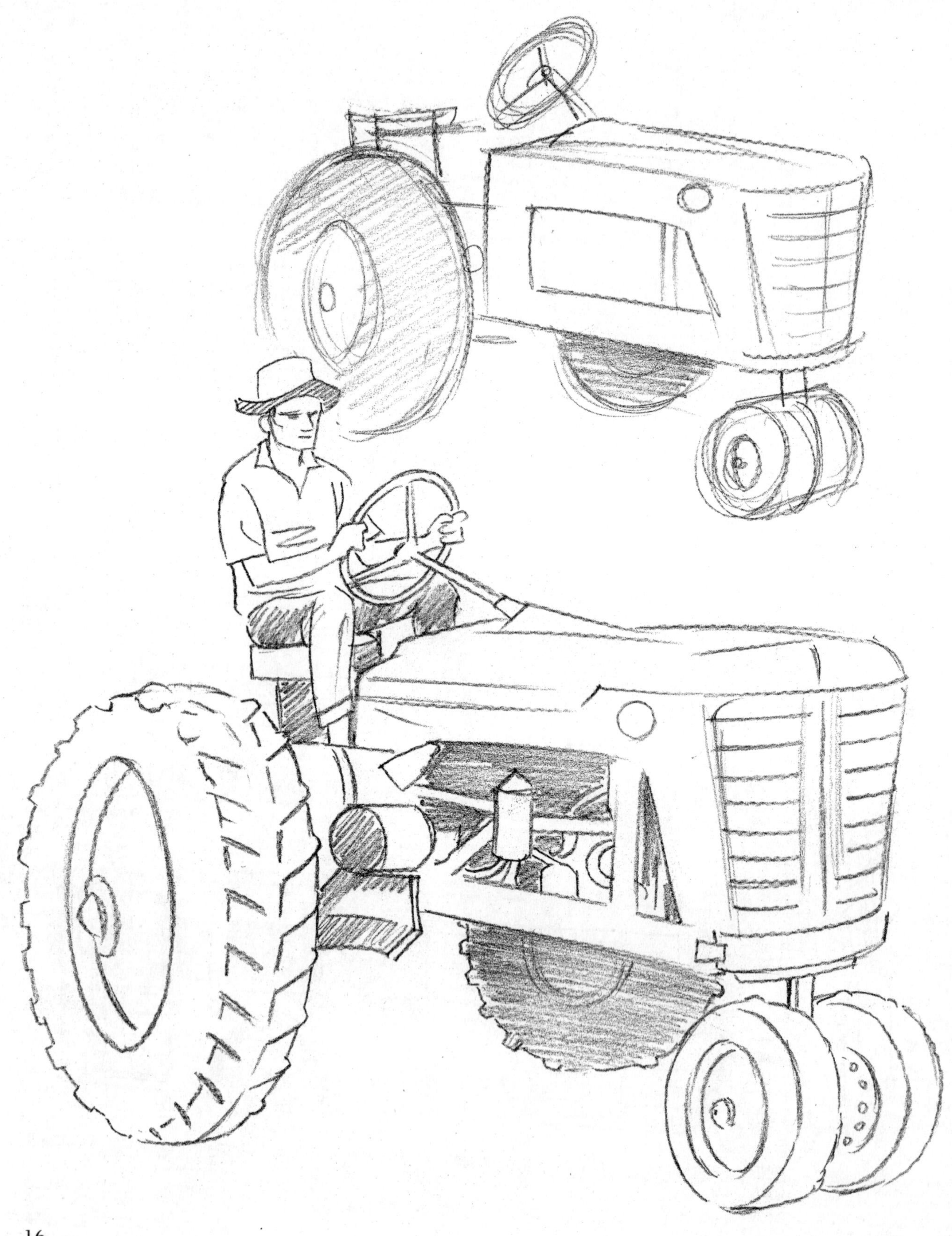

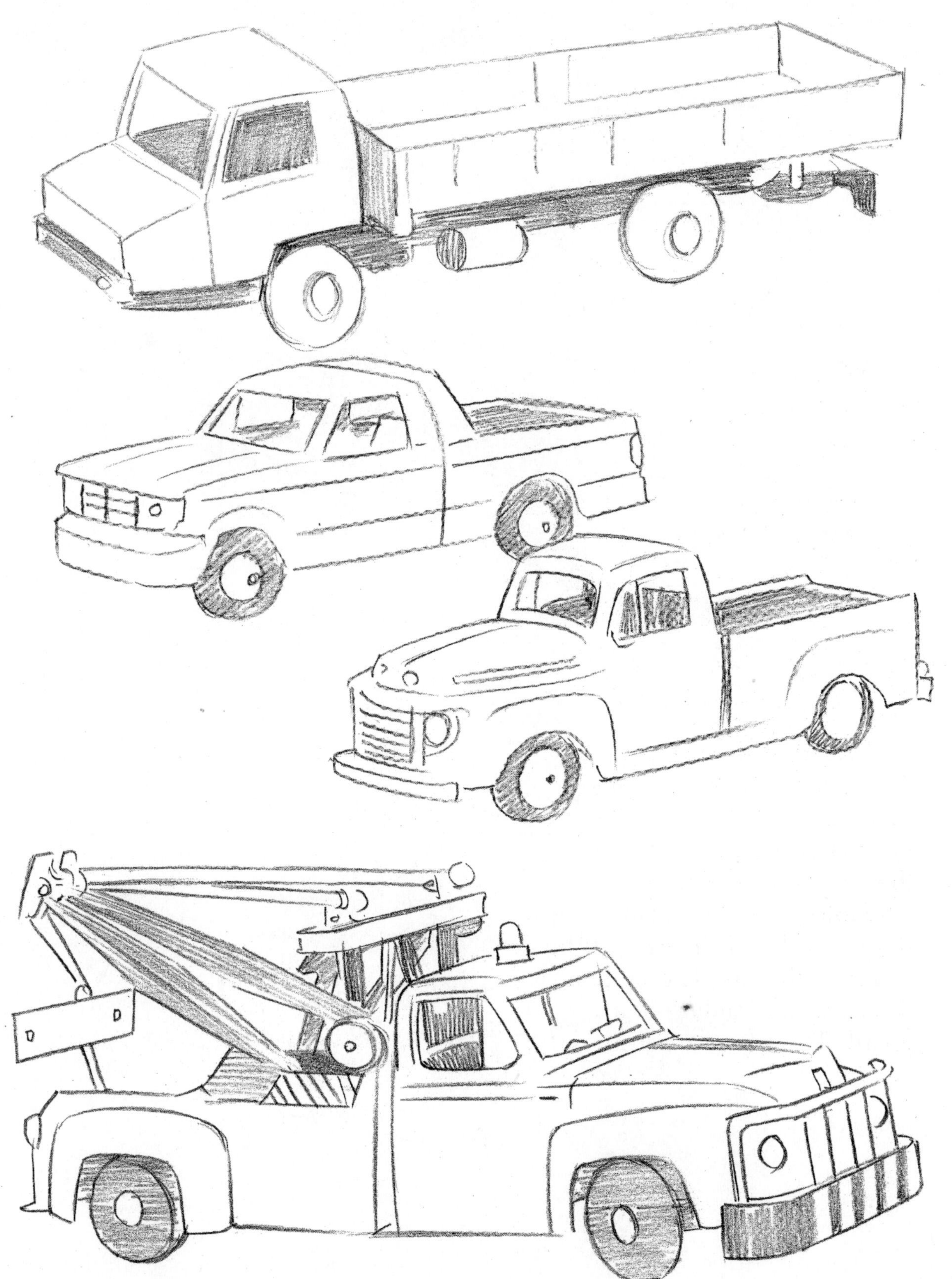

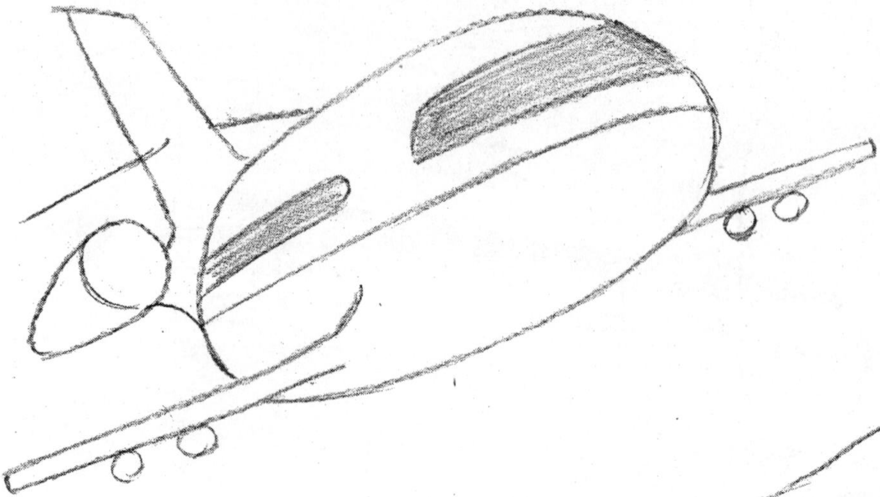

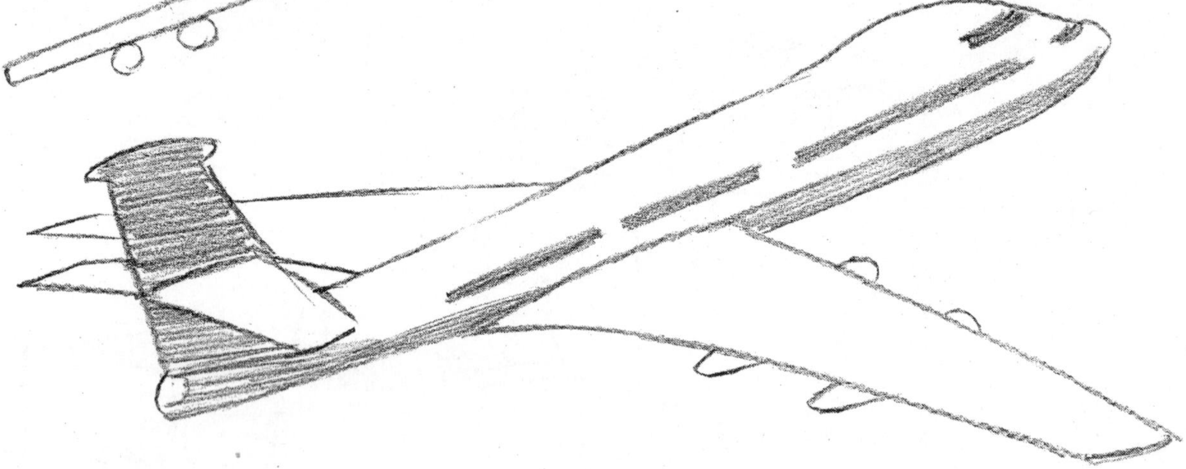

Though aeroplanes are huge, their drawings are tiny. Compared to other vehicles, they are easier to draw. Windows of an aeroplane, like those of a far-off house, can be shown with dots. The outline is similar to the outline of a gourd. The wings are just tapering stripes.

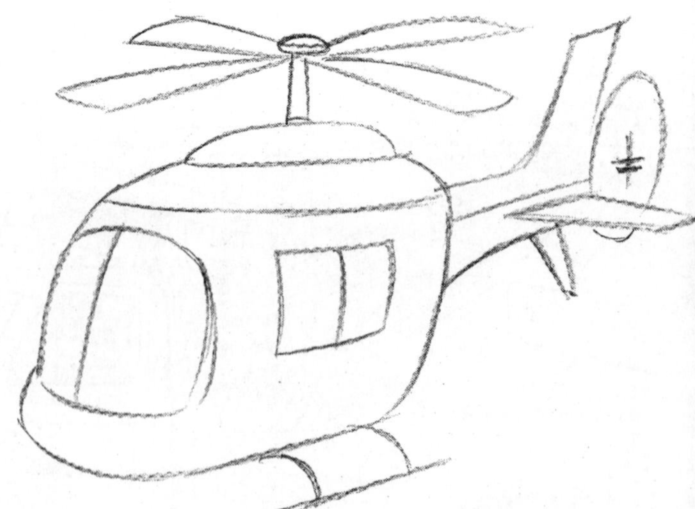

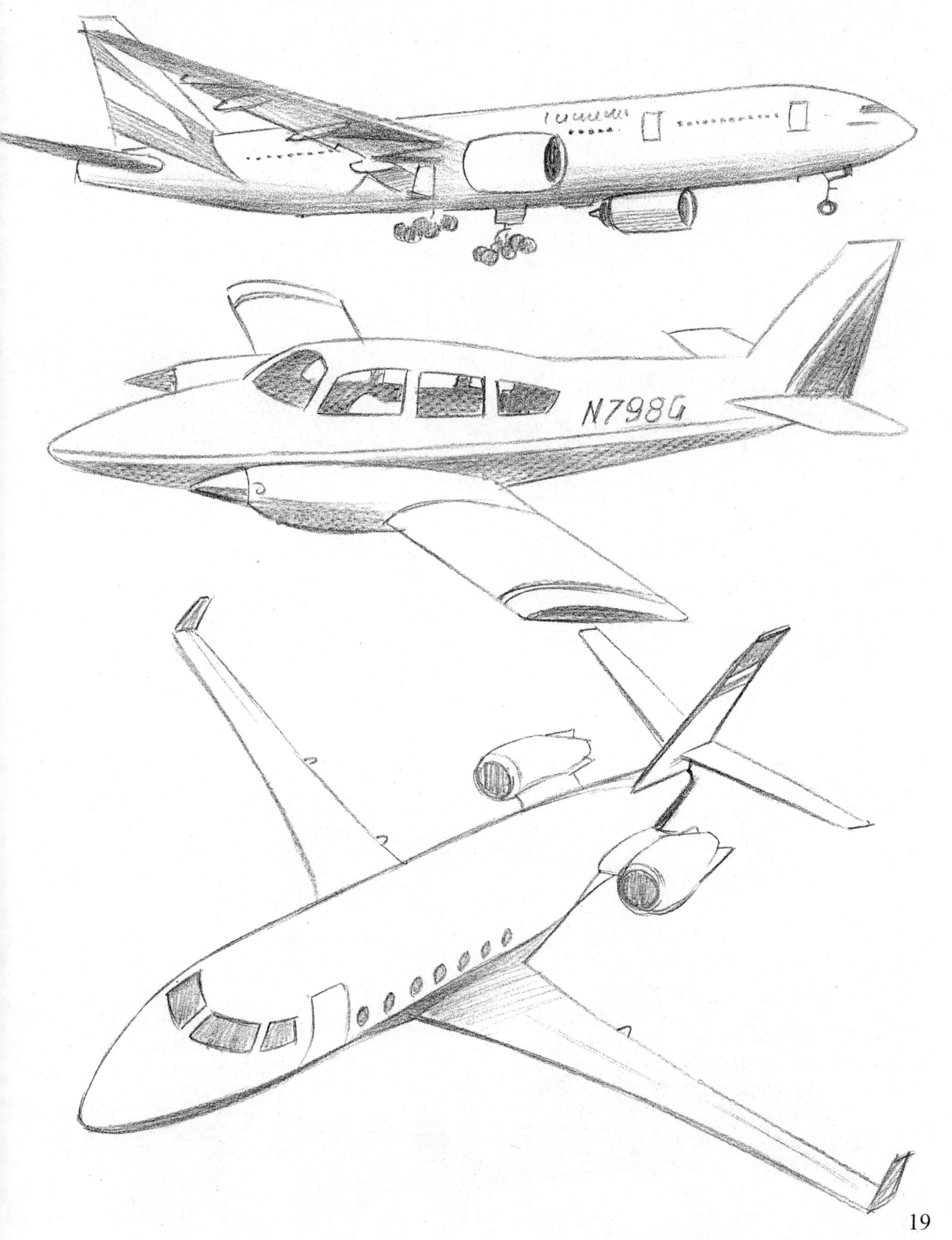
N798G

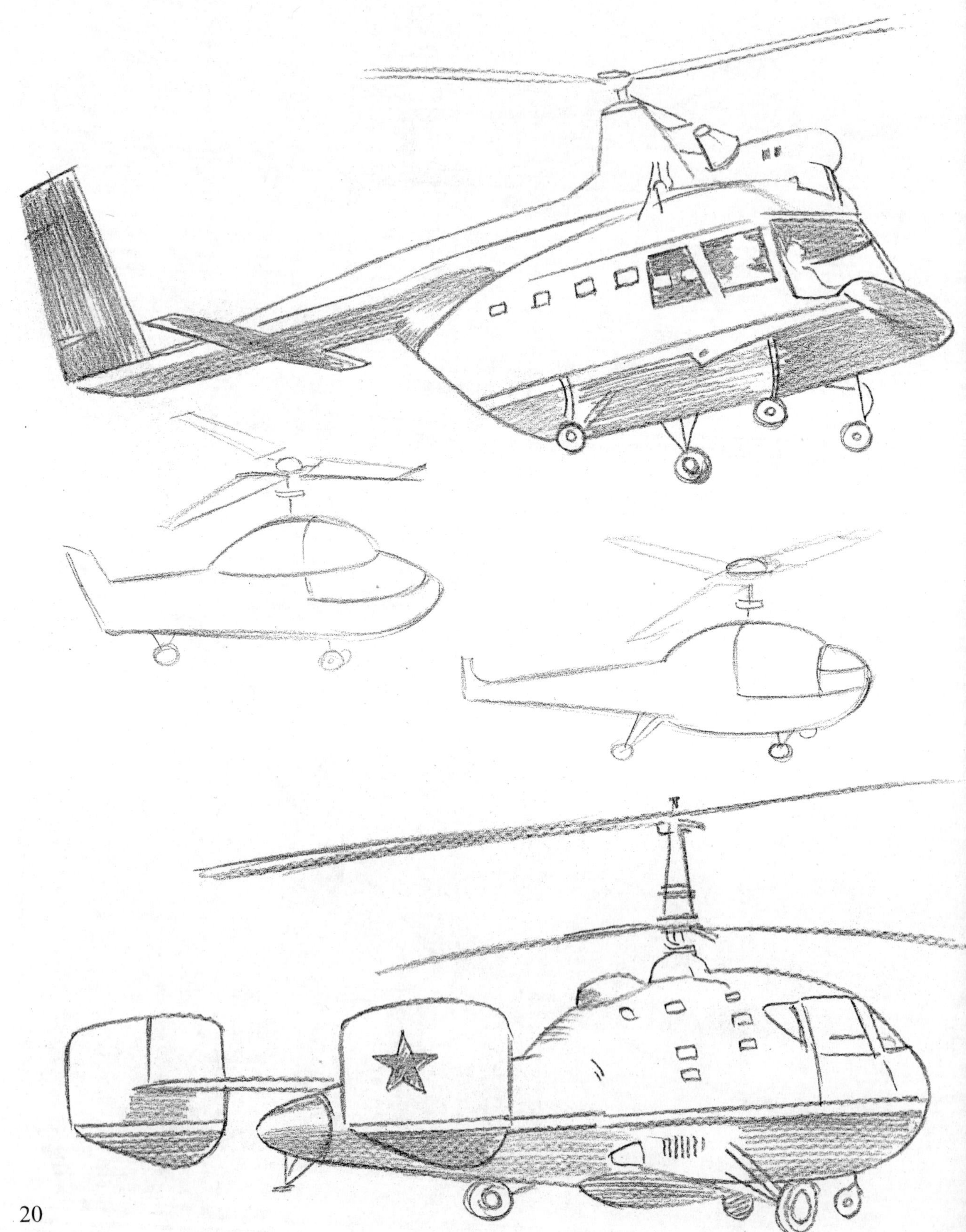

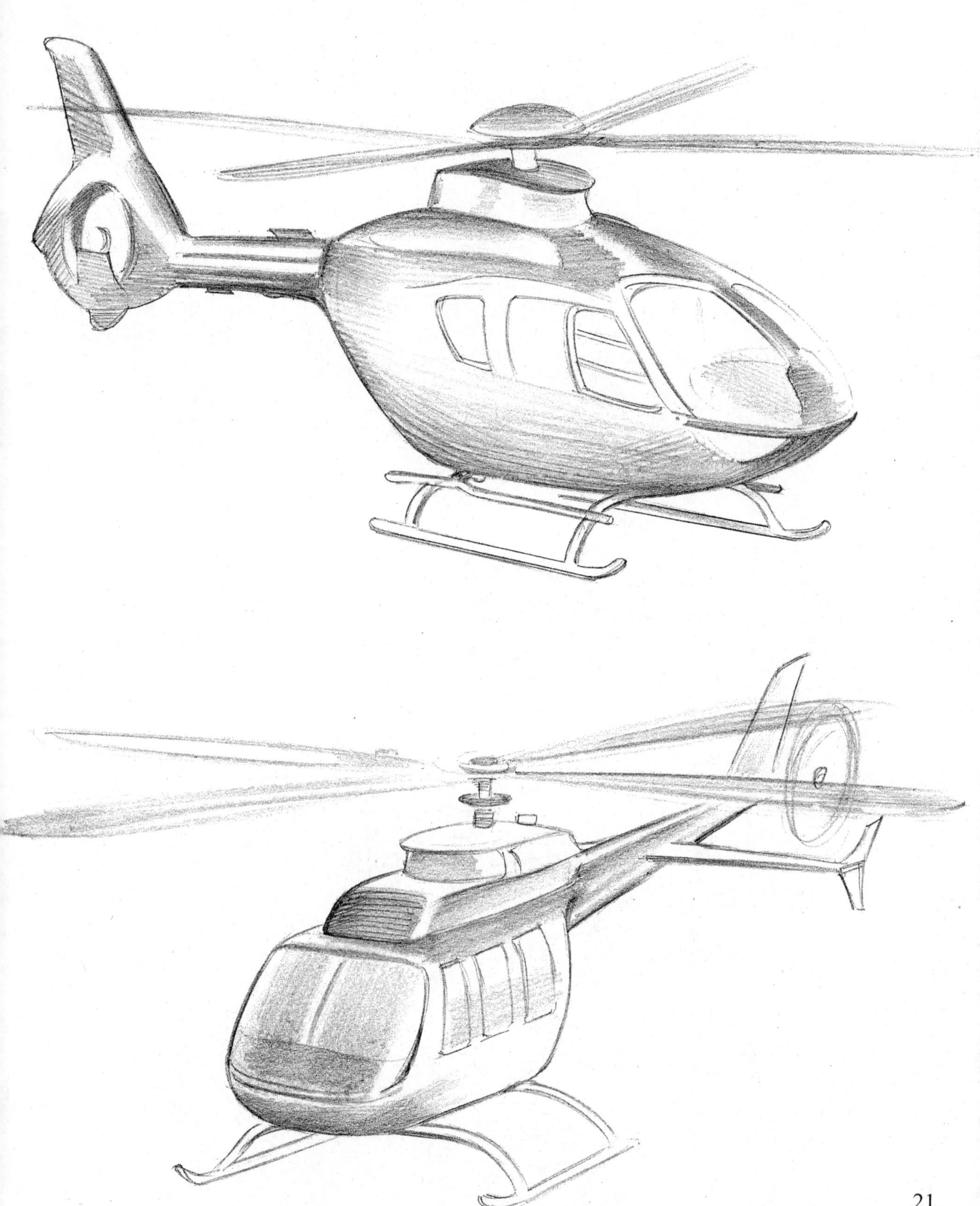

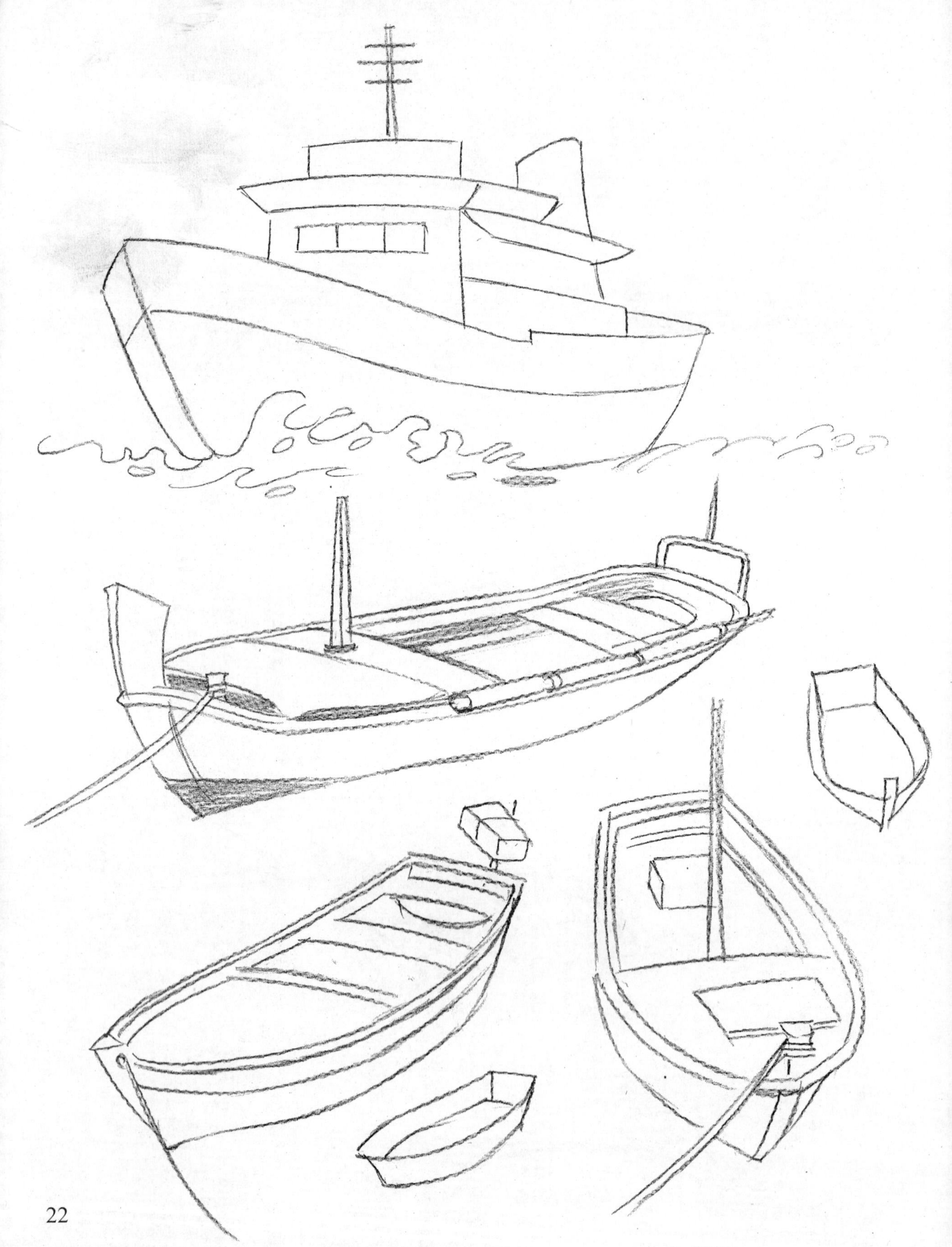

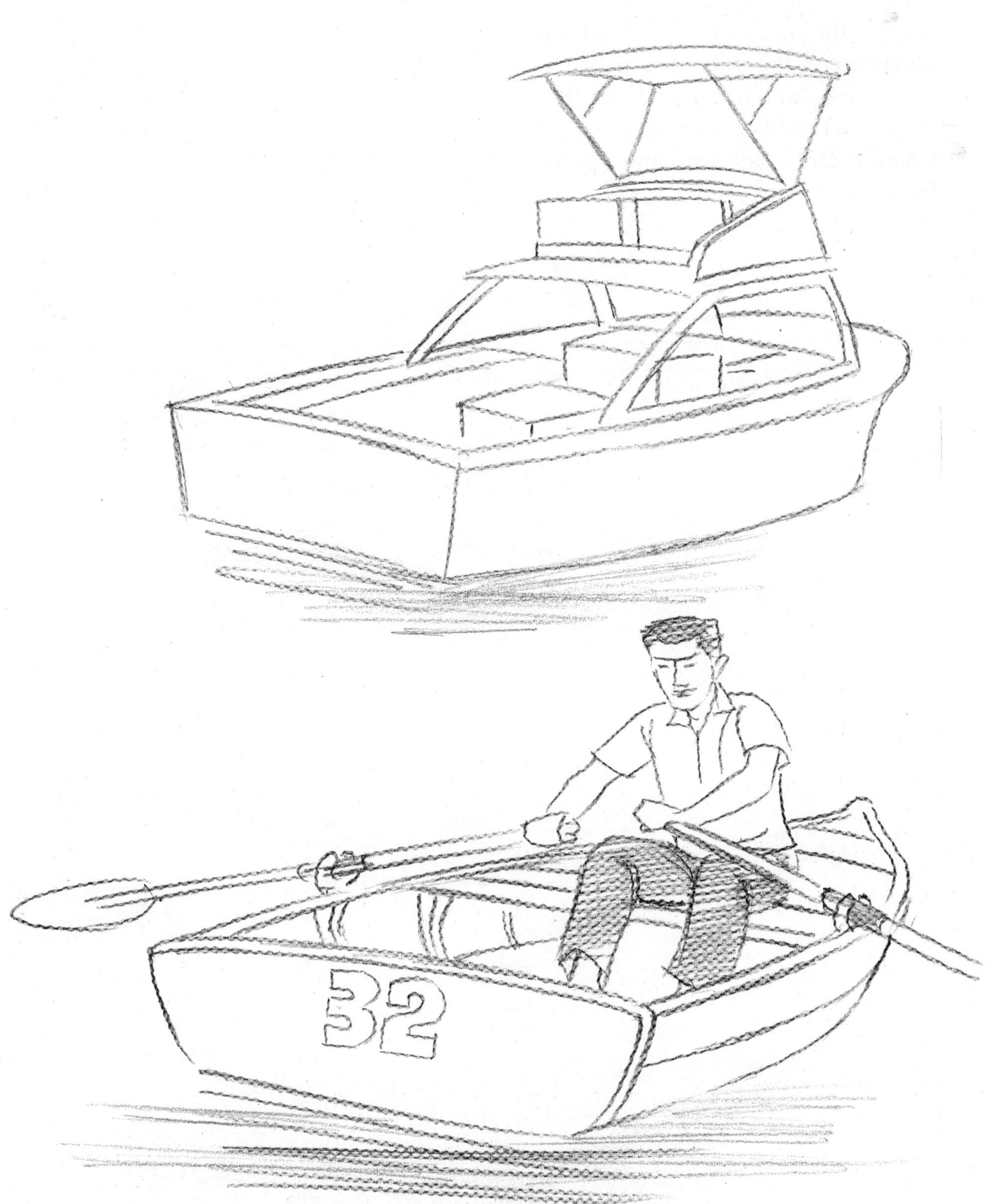
32

All bogies of a train are of the same height. But as per the principle of perspective, the engine which is closer to us looks much bigger than the bogies. These bogies seem to become smaller and smaller as they go away from us.

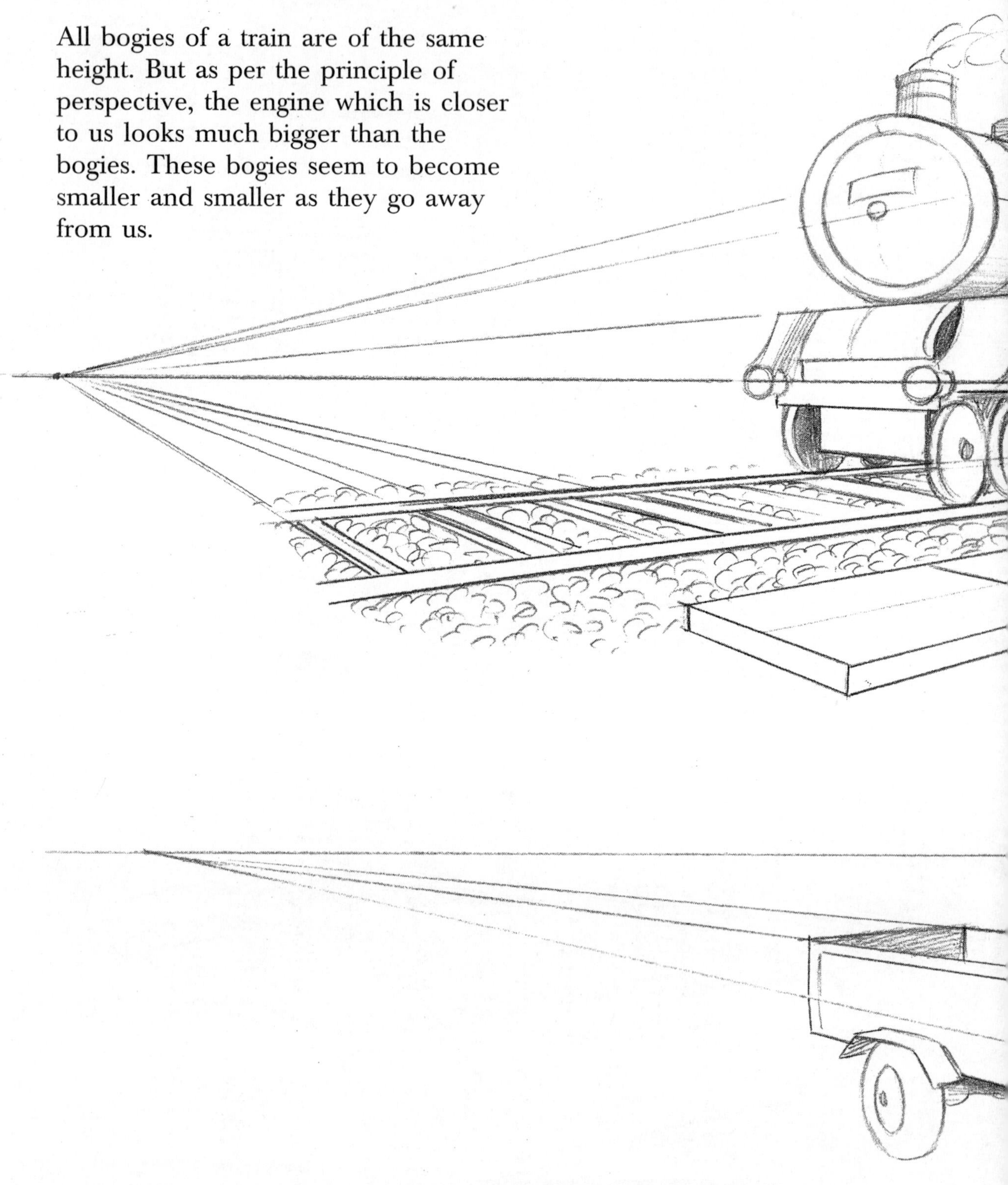

In this drawing, lines showing vanishing points are drawn, and based on these, the train is drawn. Once you know perspective well, drawing the lines of vanishing points will not be necessary.

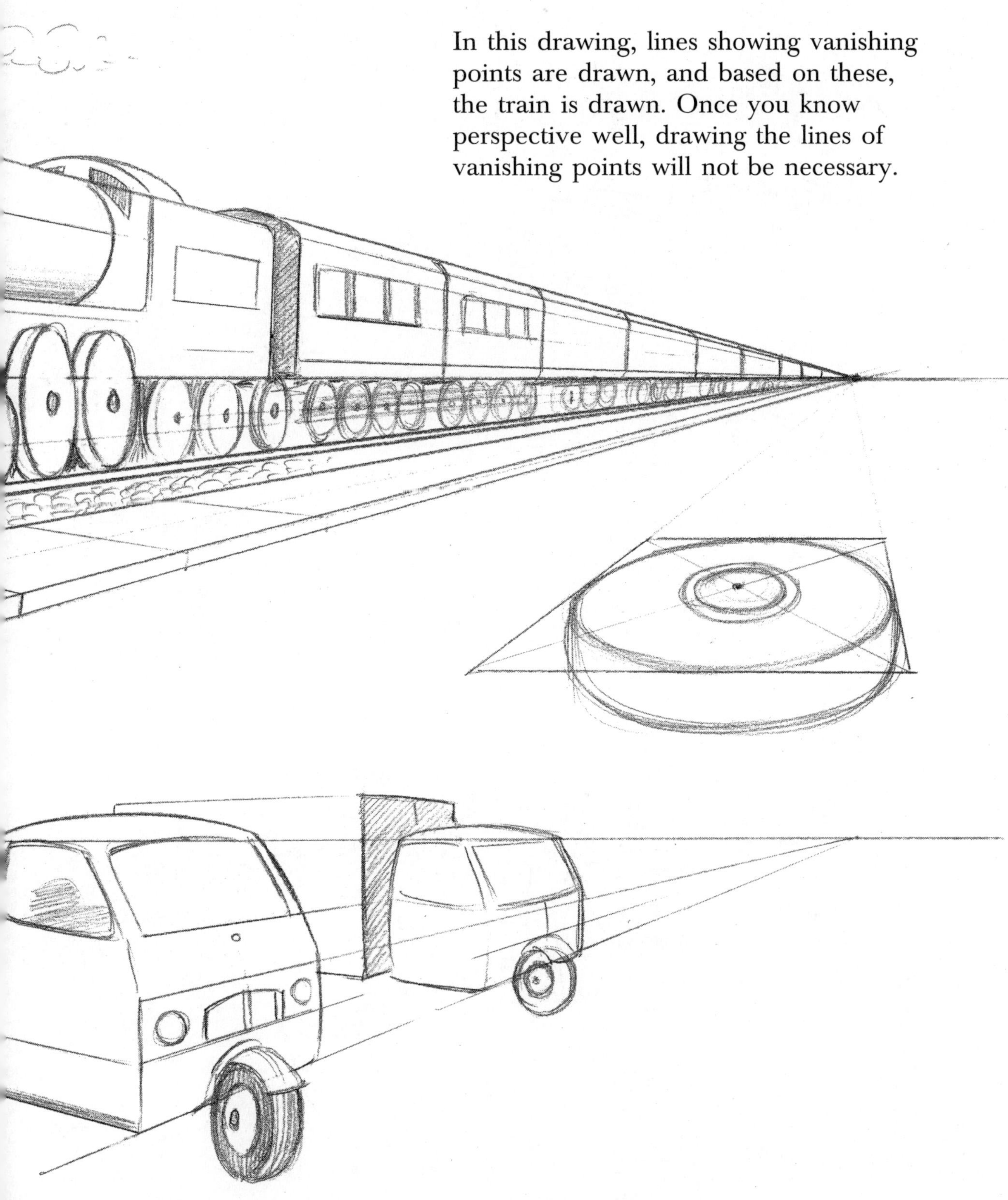

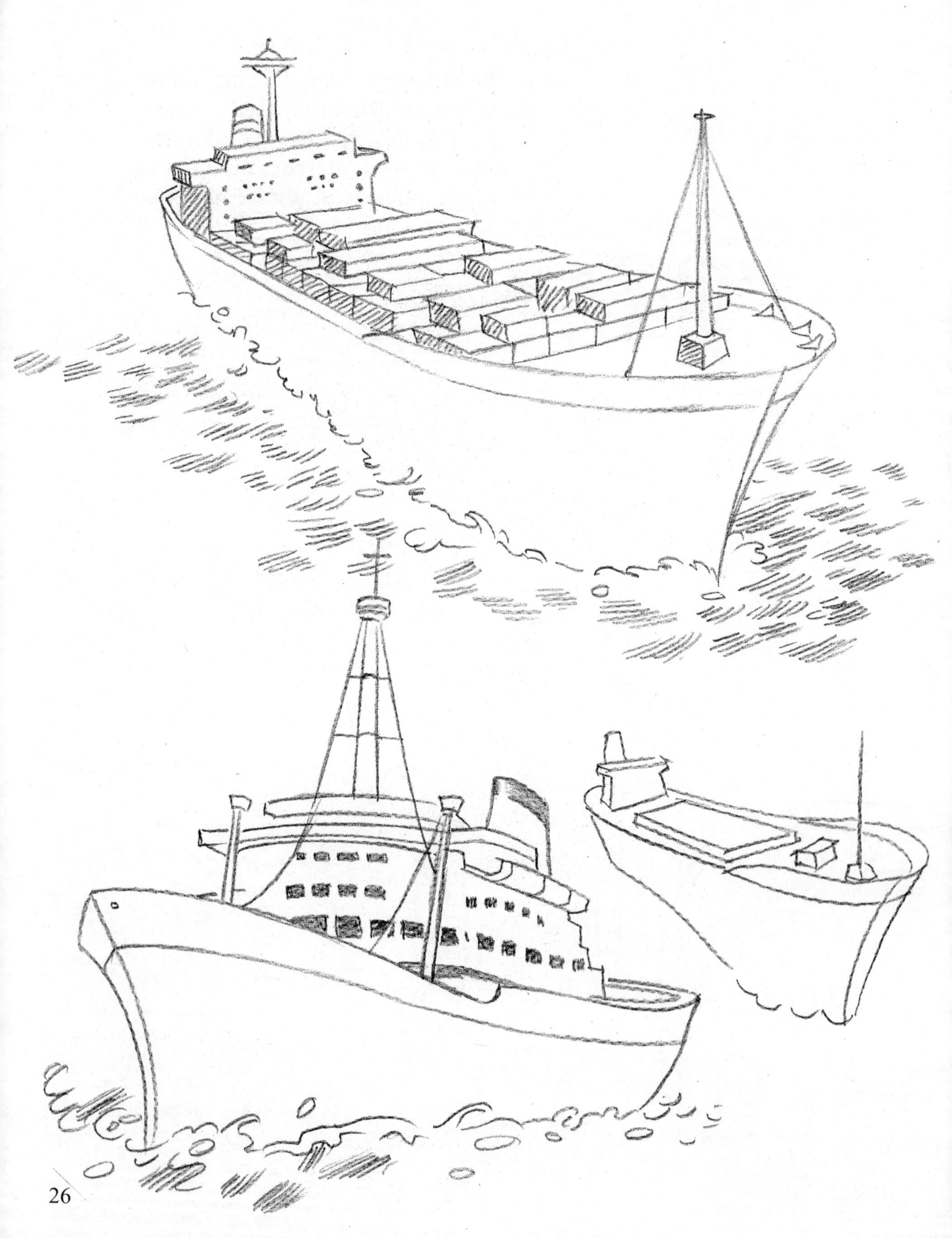

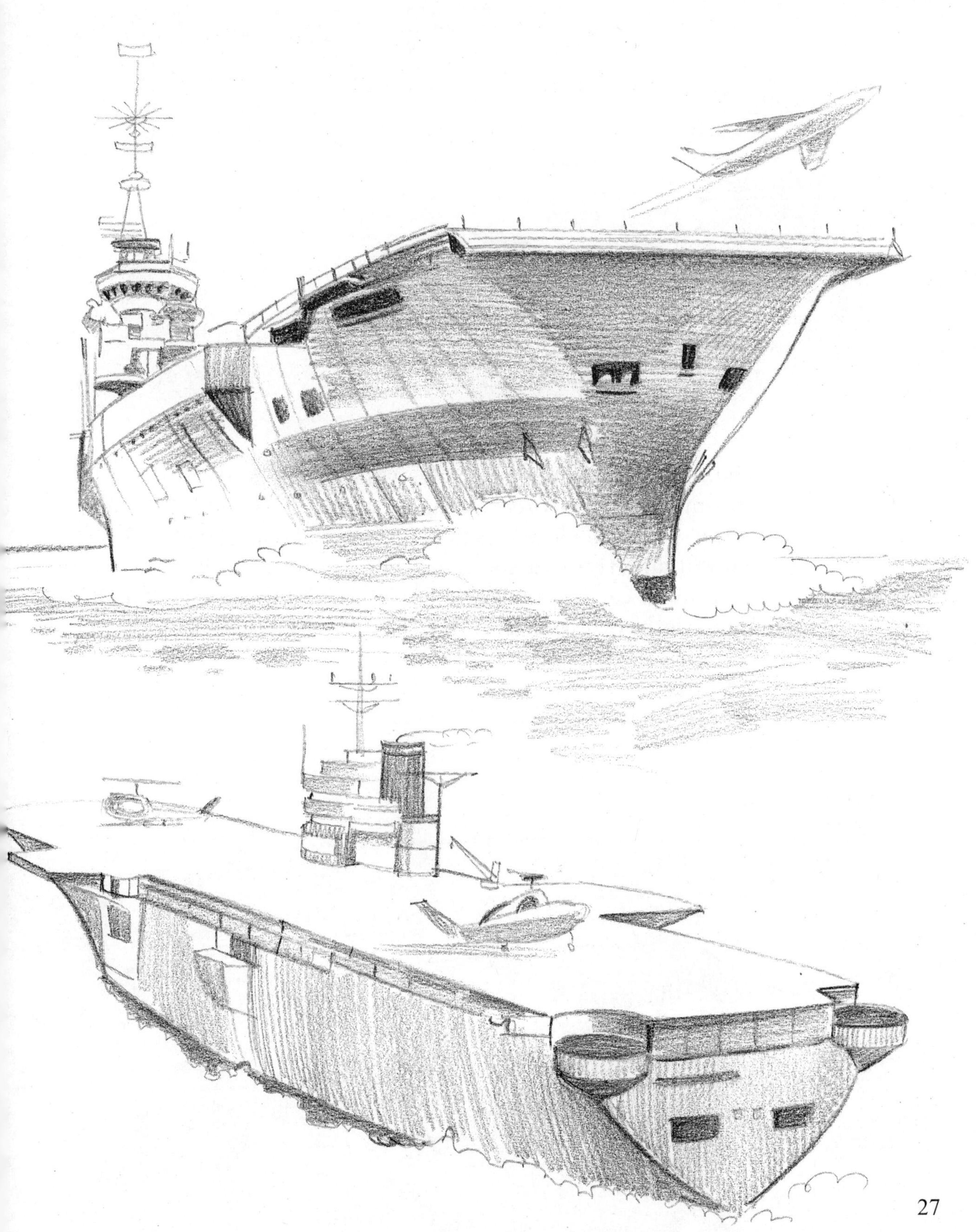

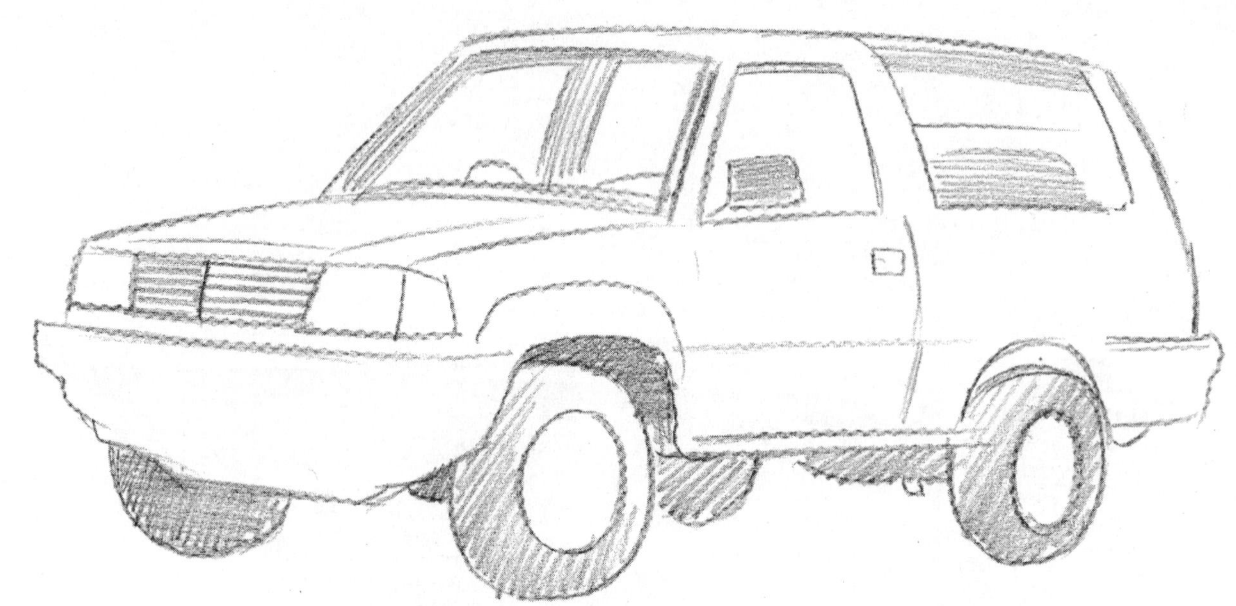

The outline of a modern car is very simple and uncomplicated. In order to understand the outline, look at the object with half-closed eyes. This way, all the details are blurred and you can see the general shape clearly.
To draw a car from various angles is slightly more difficult. Here we have given five– six drawings. These will help you in your drawings.

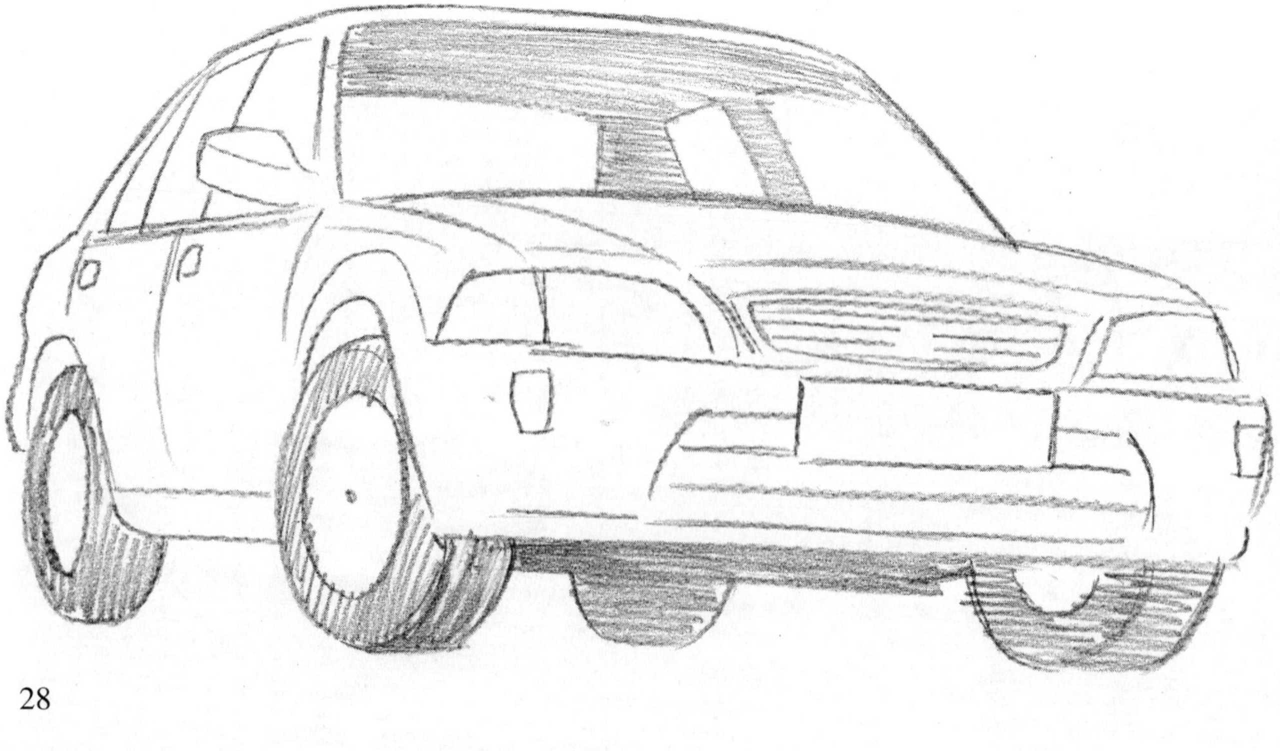

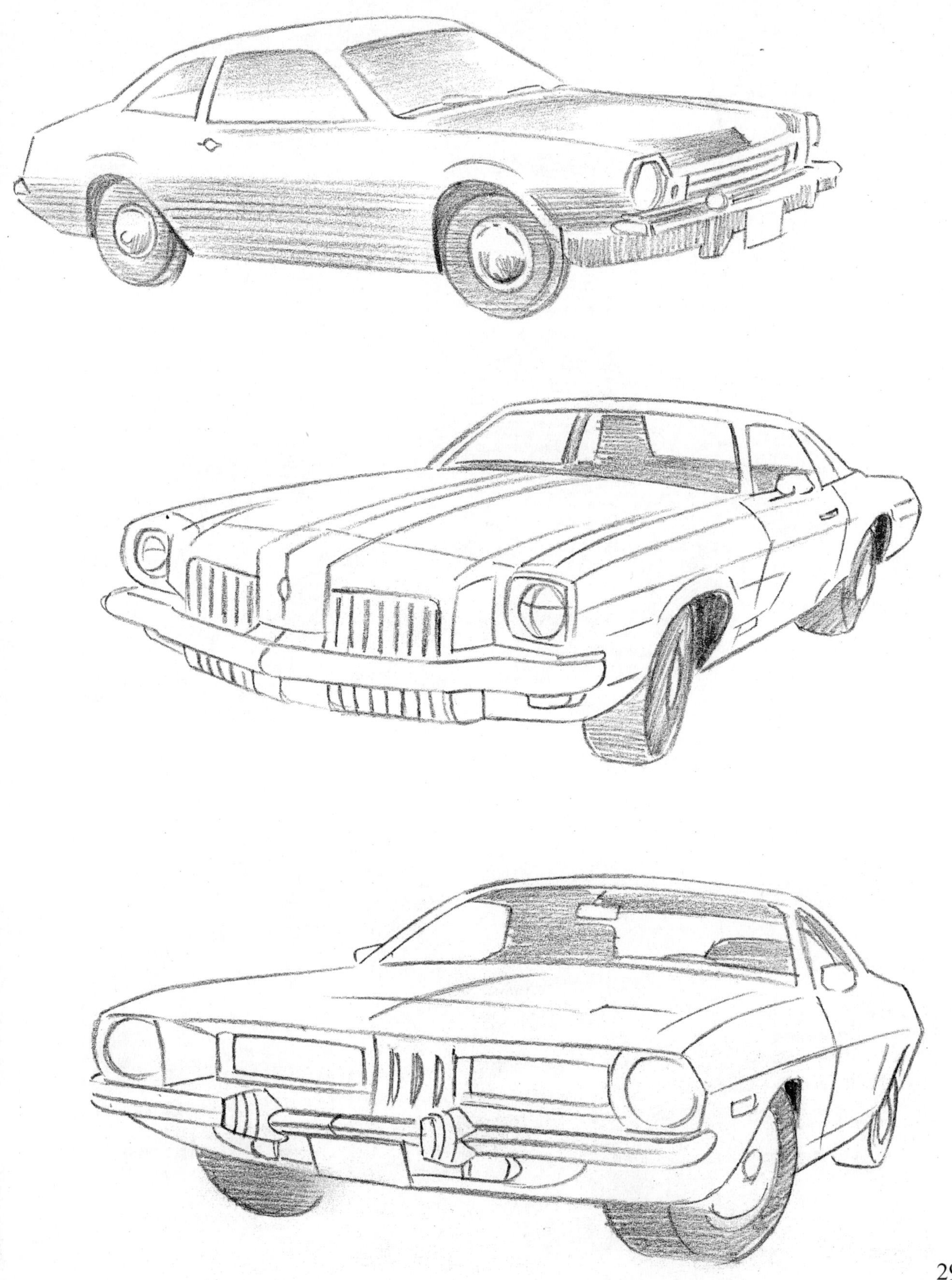

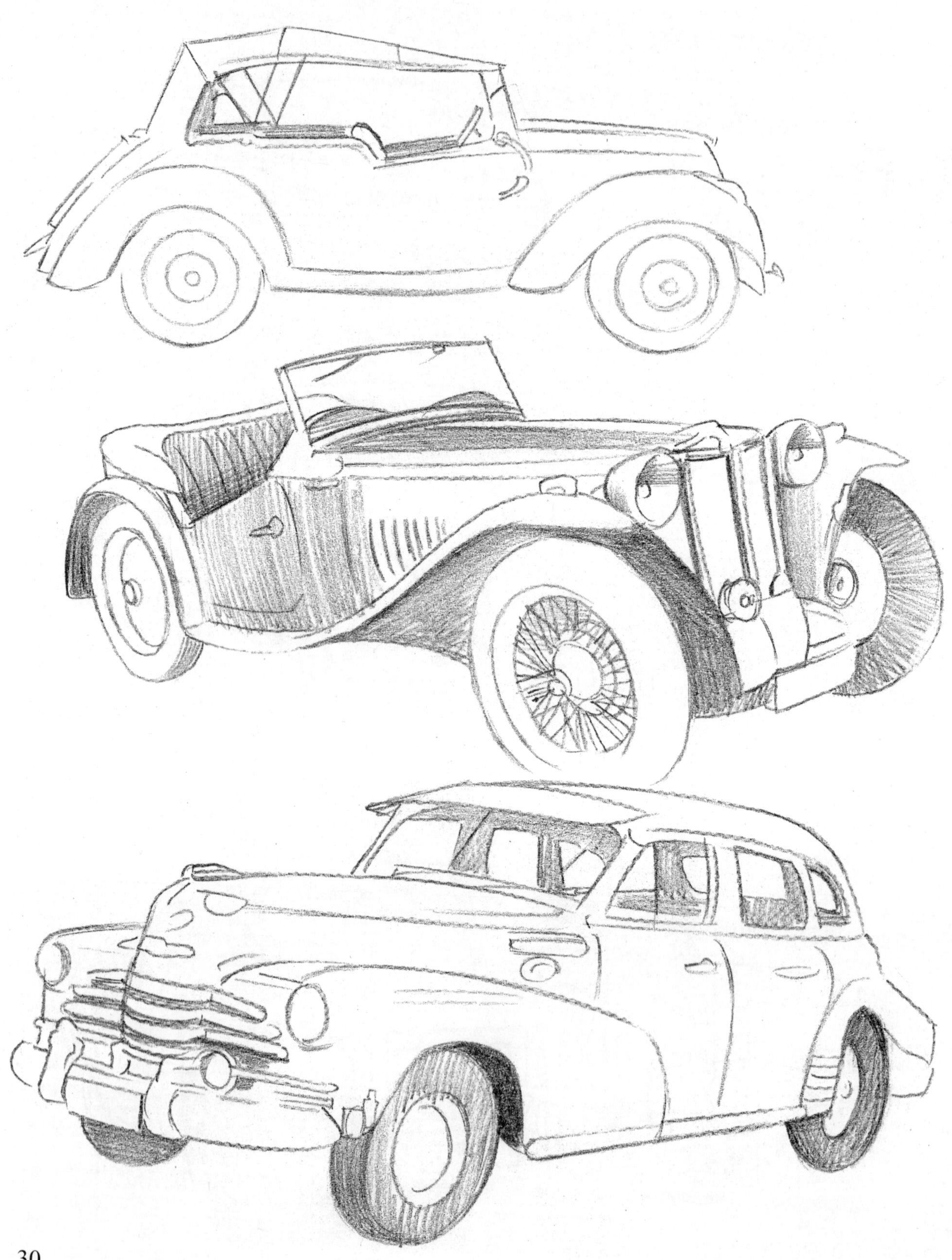

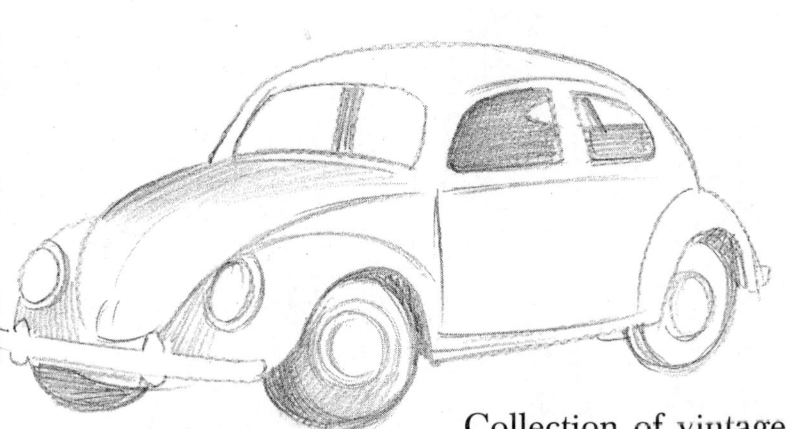

Collection of vintage cars is a costly affair and only the rich can afford it. But anyone can draw these cars and gain pleasure. These cars are very beautiful. Sometimes exhibitions or rallies of these cars are arranged. Also, special magazines for vehicles publish their photographs. Either from actual observations or from such photographs, you can practise drawing and painting such vintage cars.

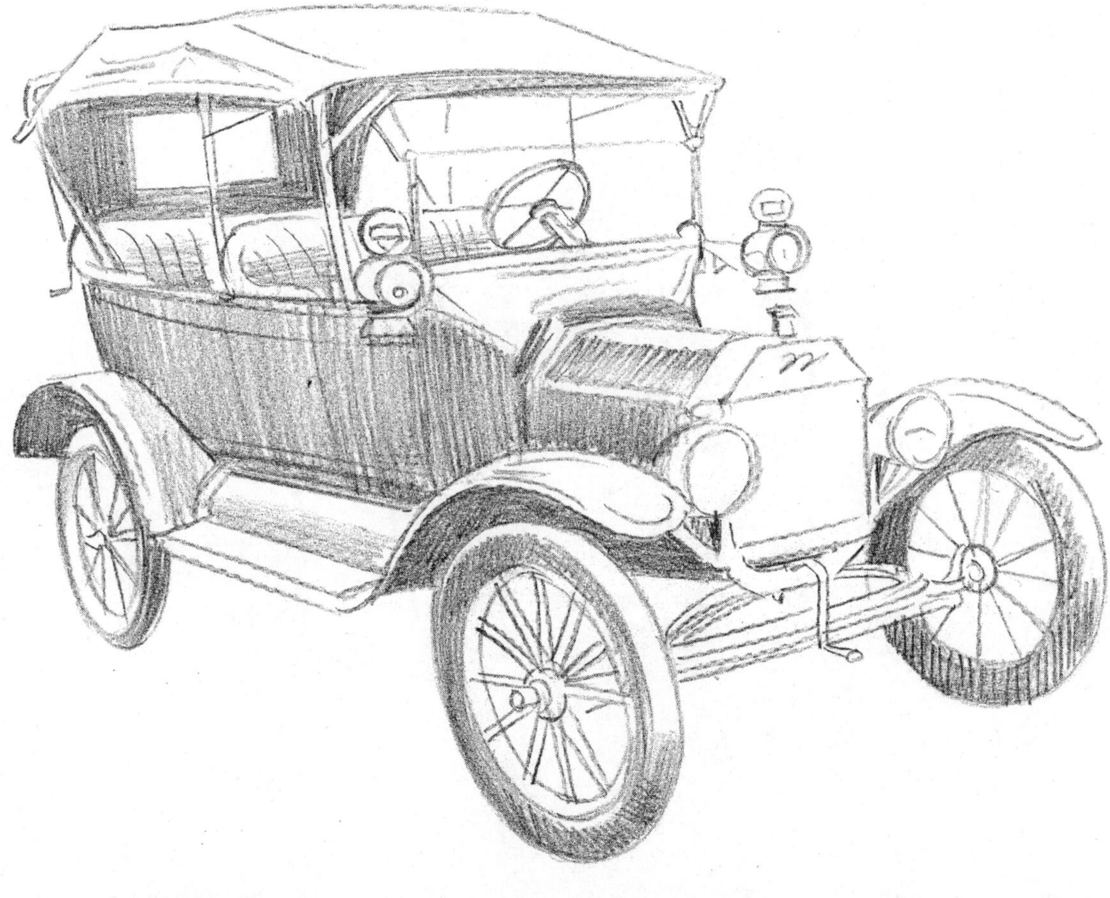

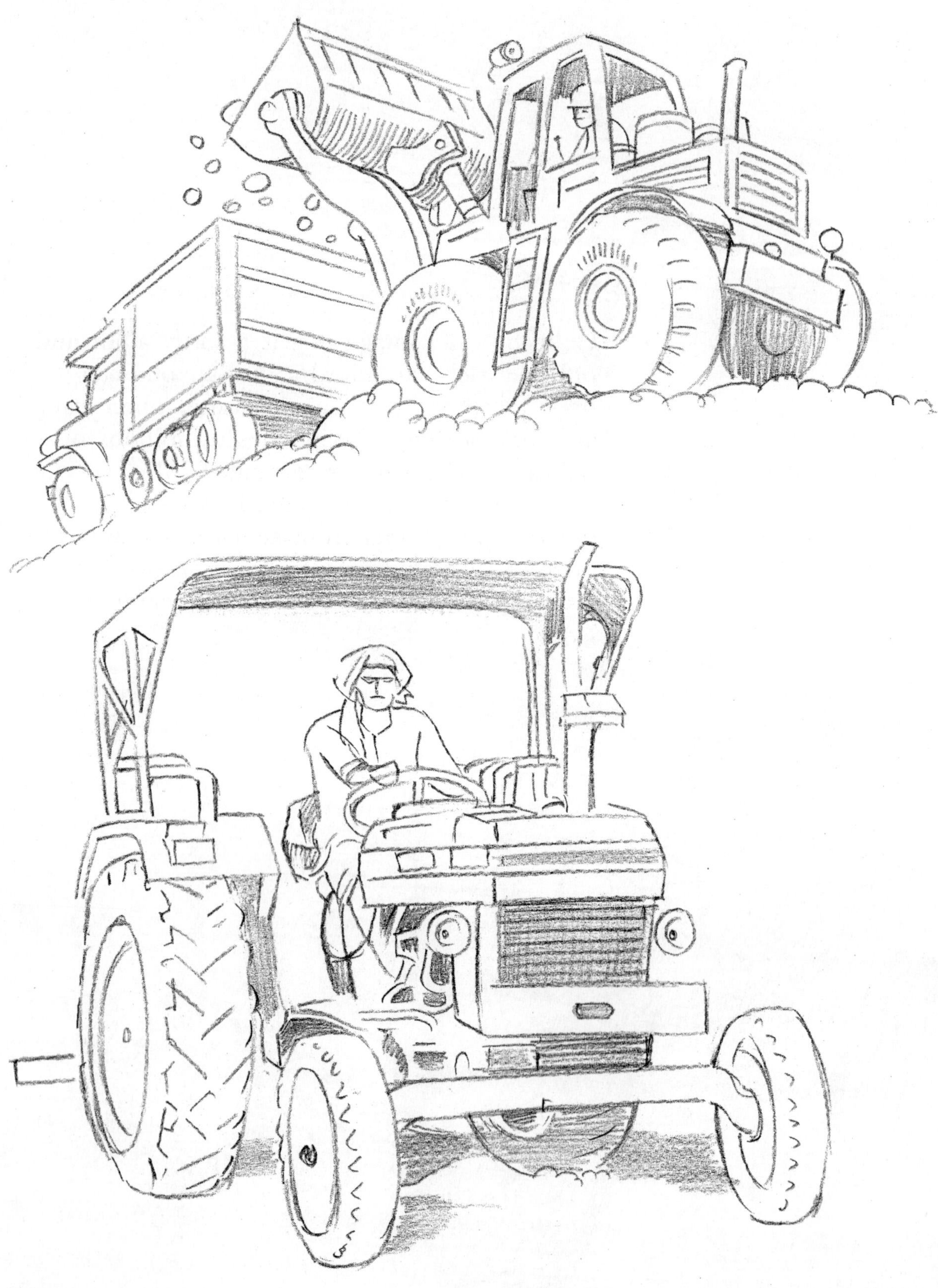

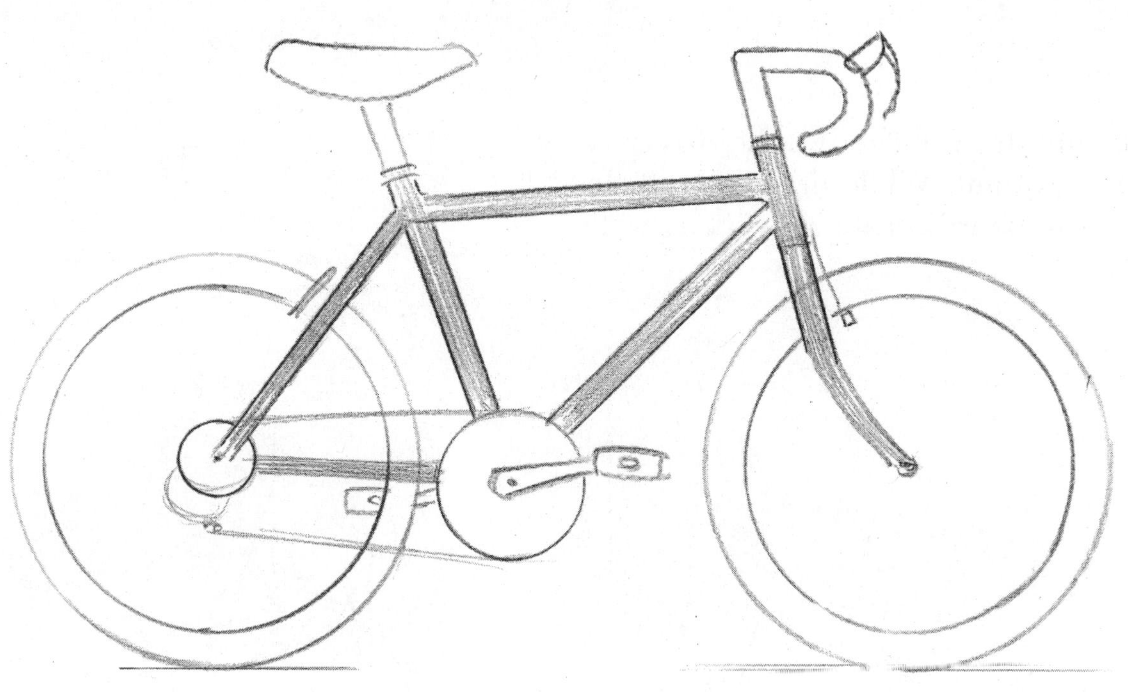

Drawing a bicycle is nothing but arranging a few geometrical forms. Draw two wheels of the same size. The distance between them should be roughly equal to the radius of a wheel. Then draw a triangle inbetween and complete the frame. Now draw the handle, seat and paddles and the bicycle is ready.

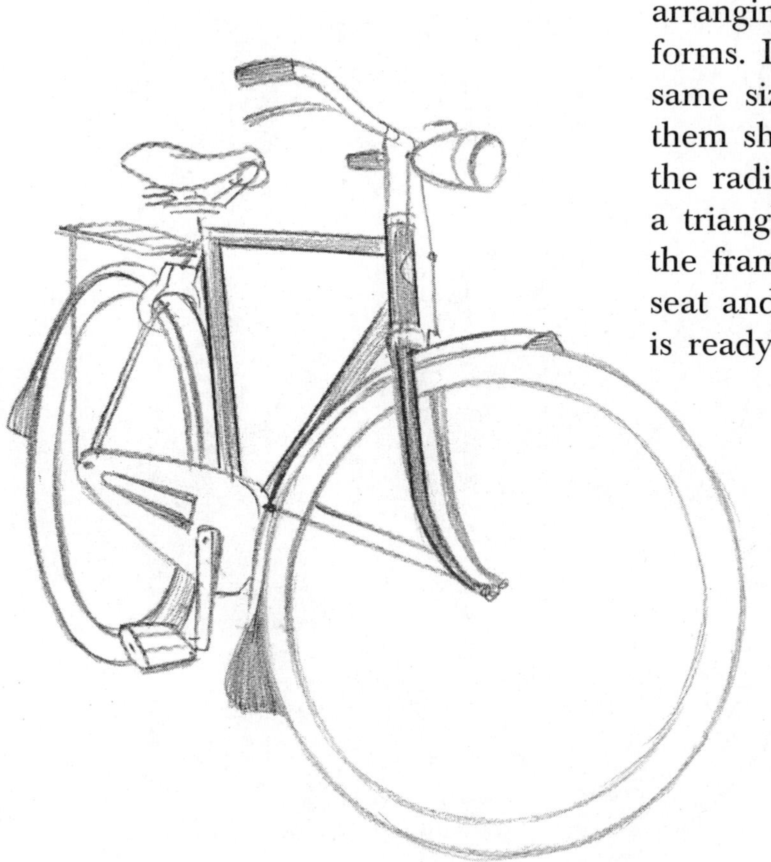

Not only the vehicle, but the driver is also important. While drawing vehicles, draw the figures of the drivers as well.

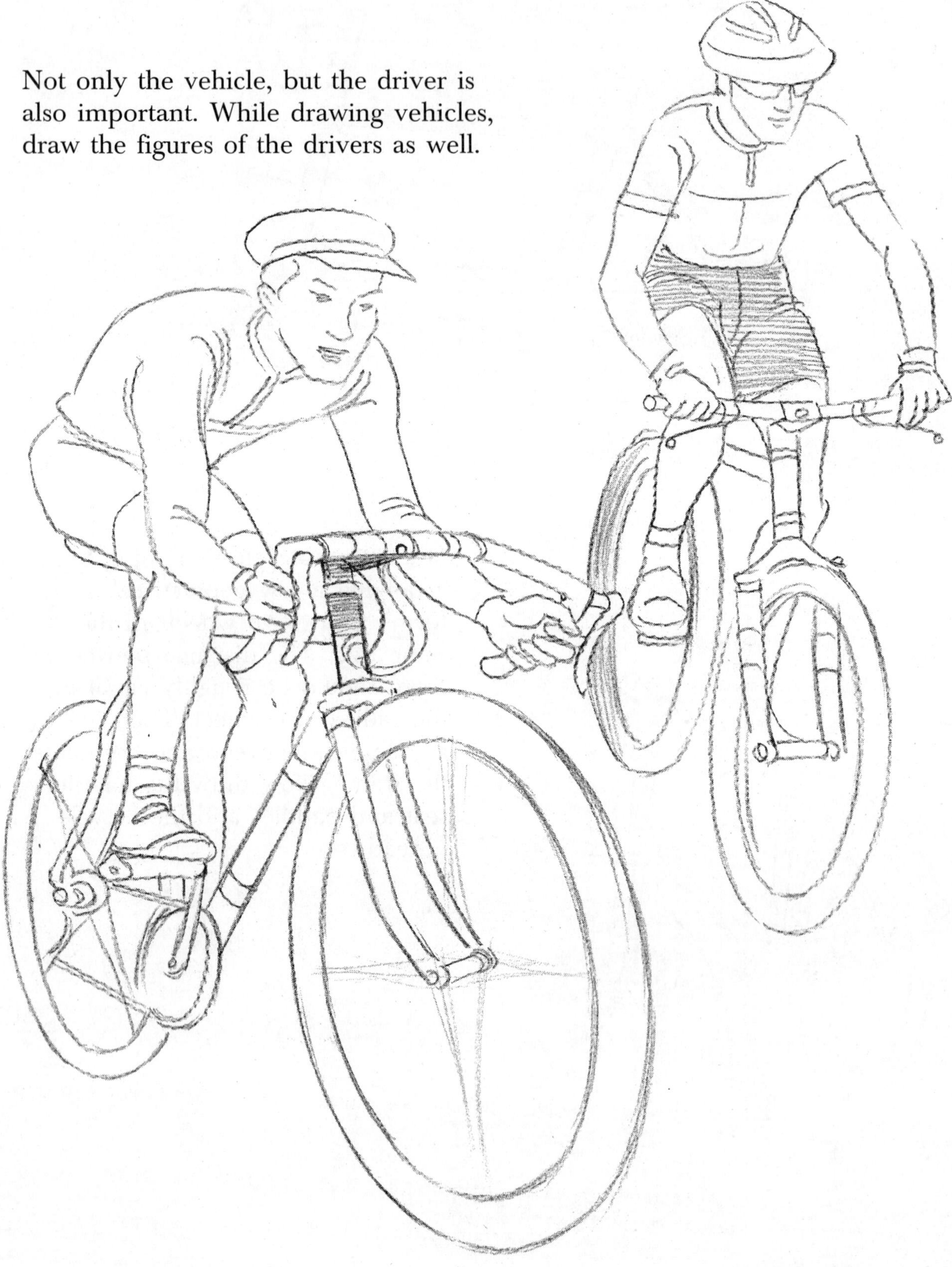

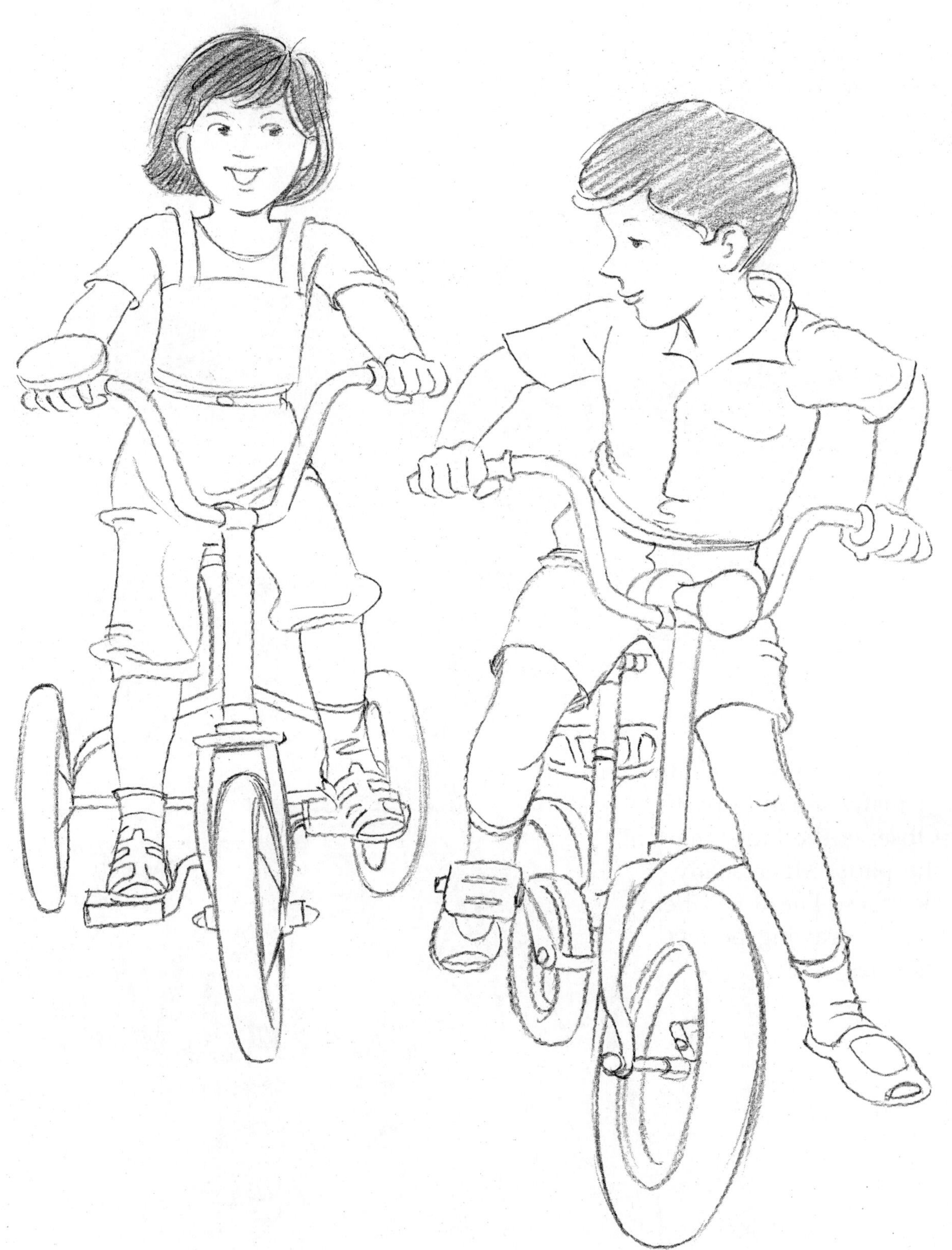

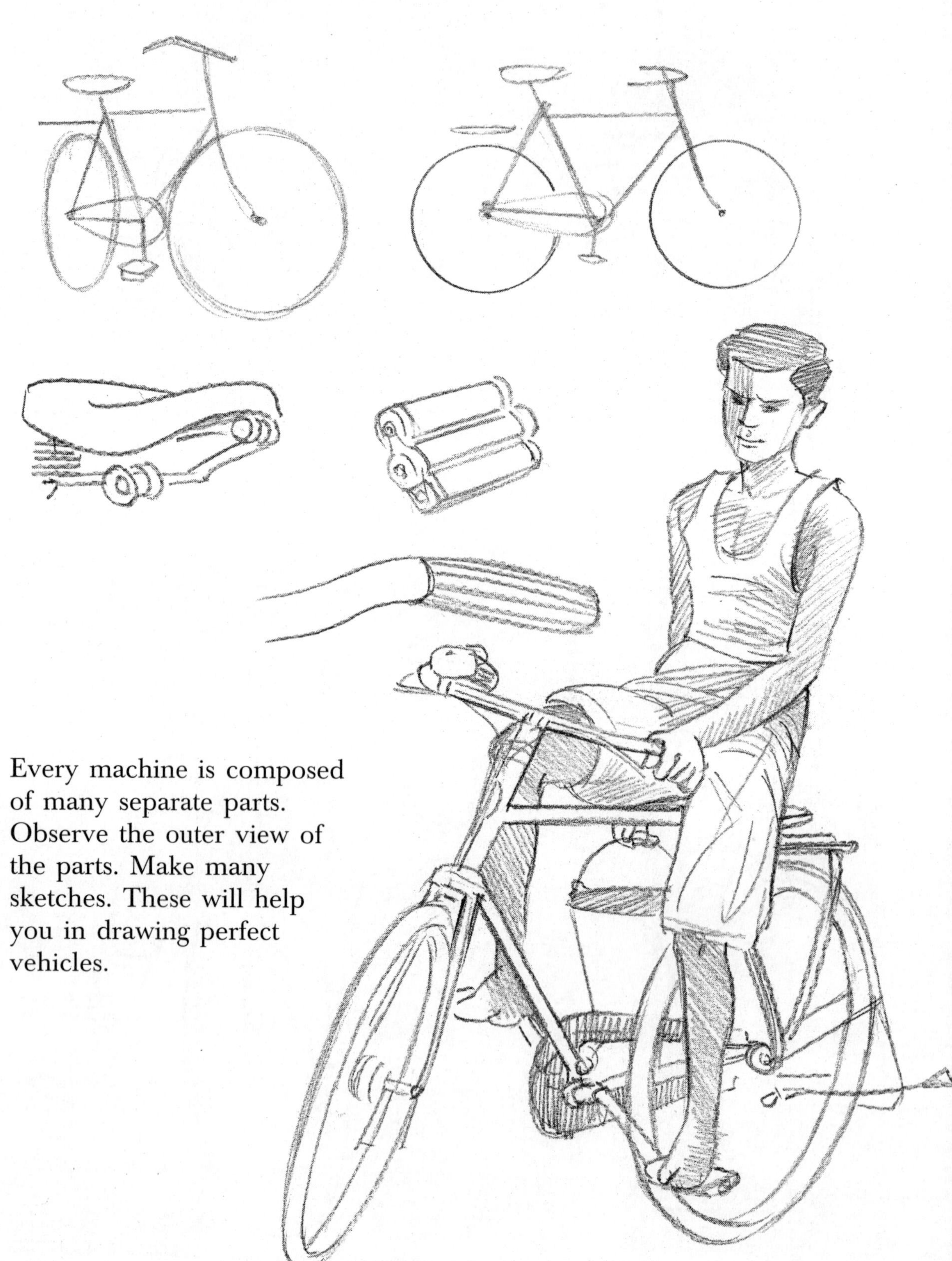

Every machine is composed of many separate parts. Observe the outer view of the parts. Make many sketches. These will help you in drawing perfect vehicles.

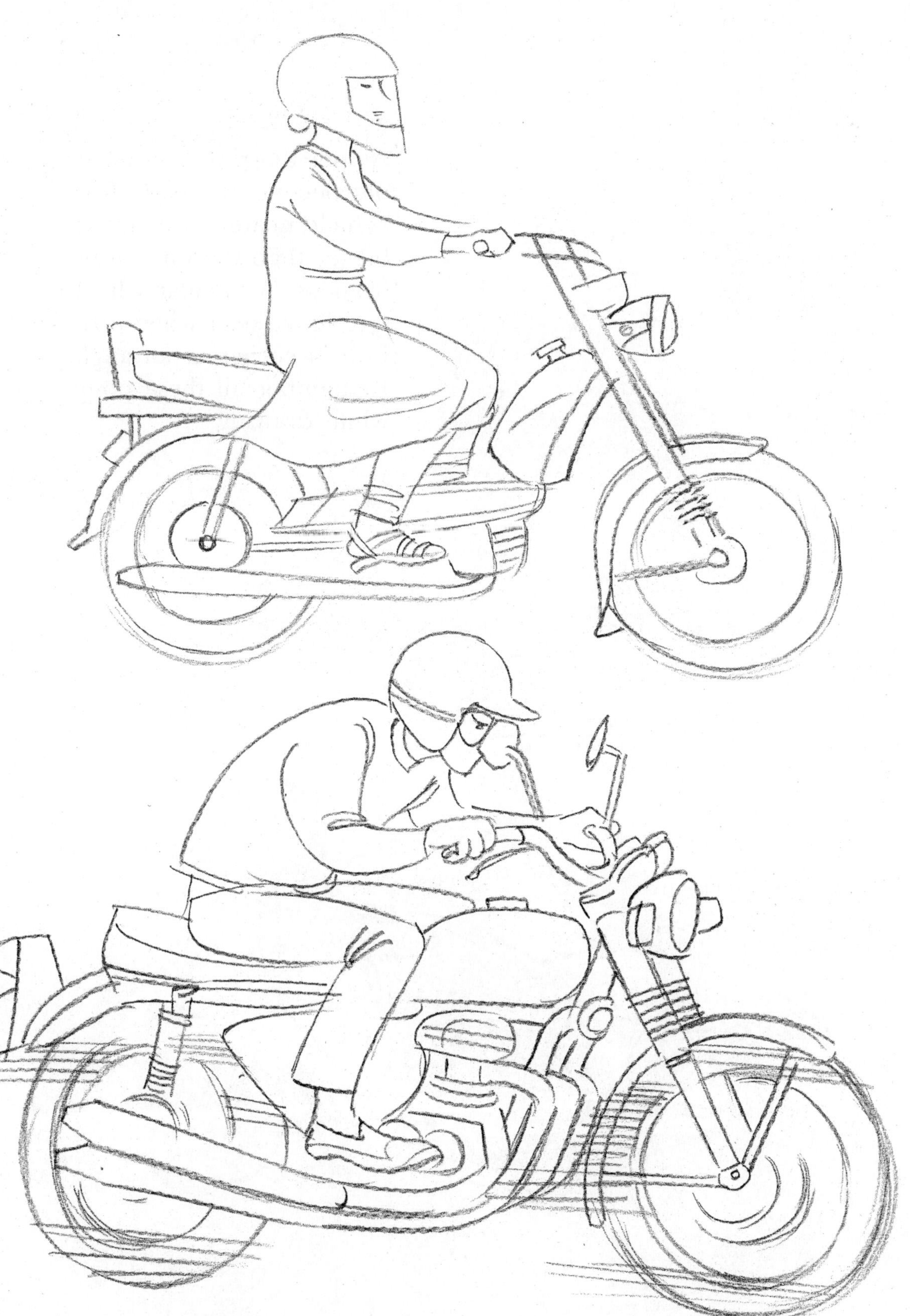

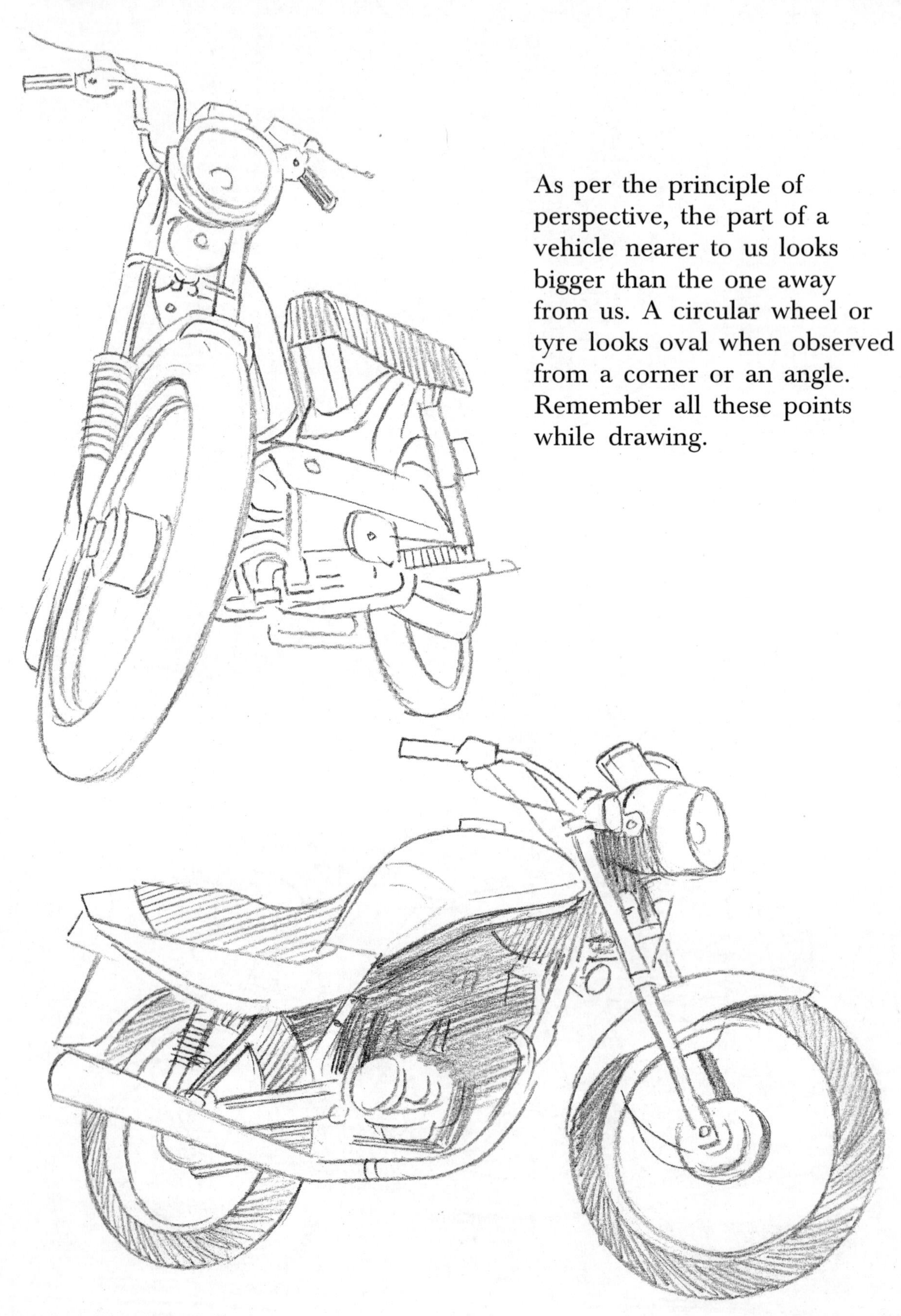

As per the principle of perspective, the part of a vehicle nearer to us looks bigger than the one away from us. A circular wheel or tyre looks oval when observed from a corner or an angle. Remember all these points while drawing.

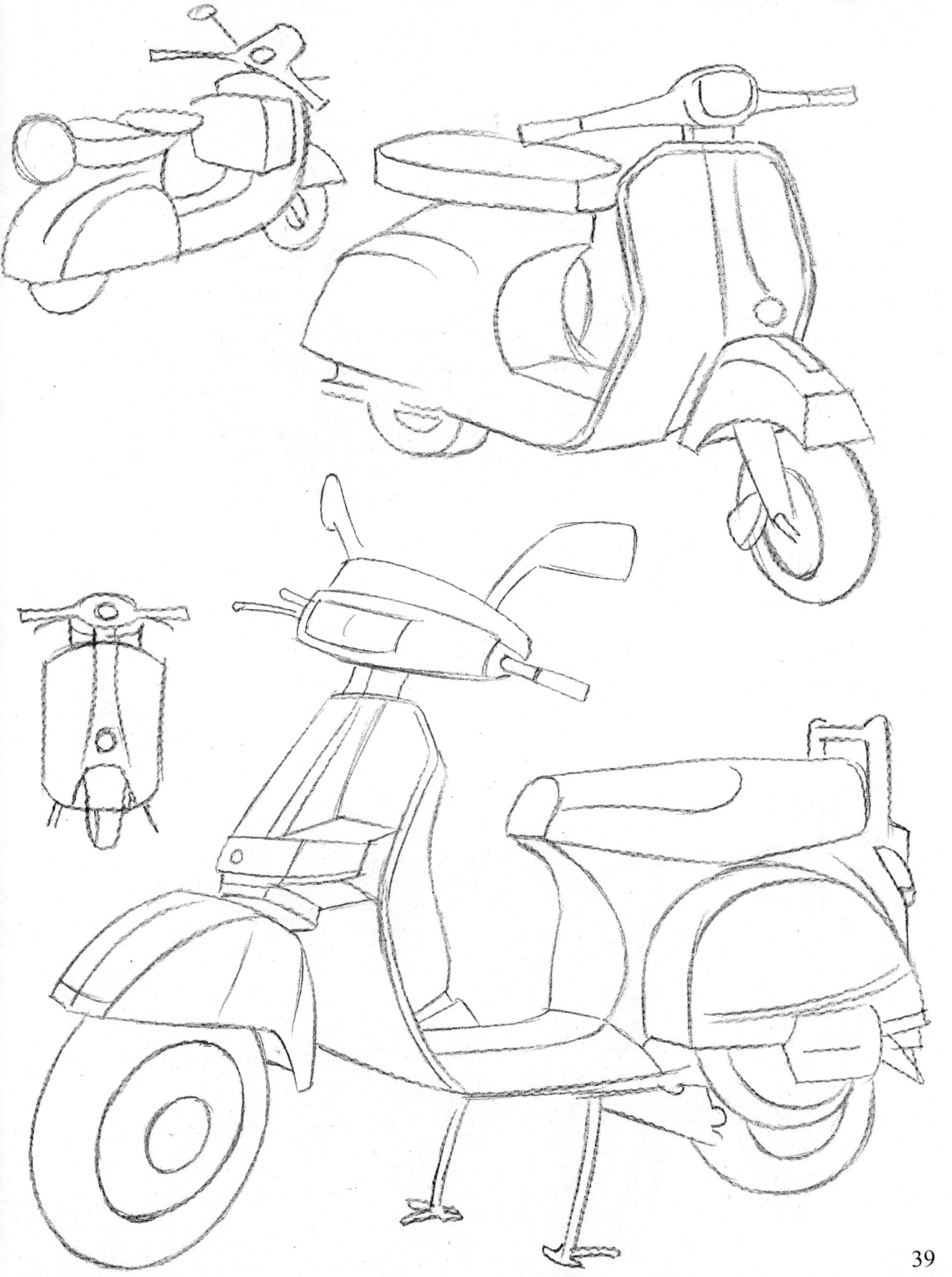

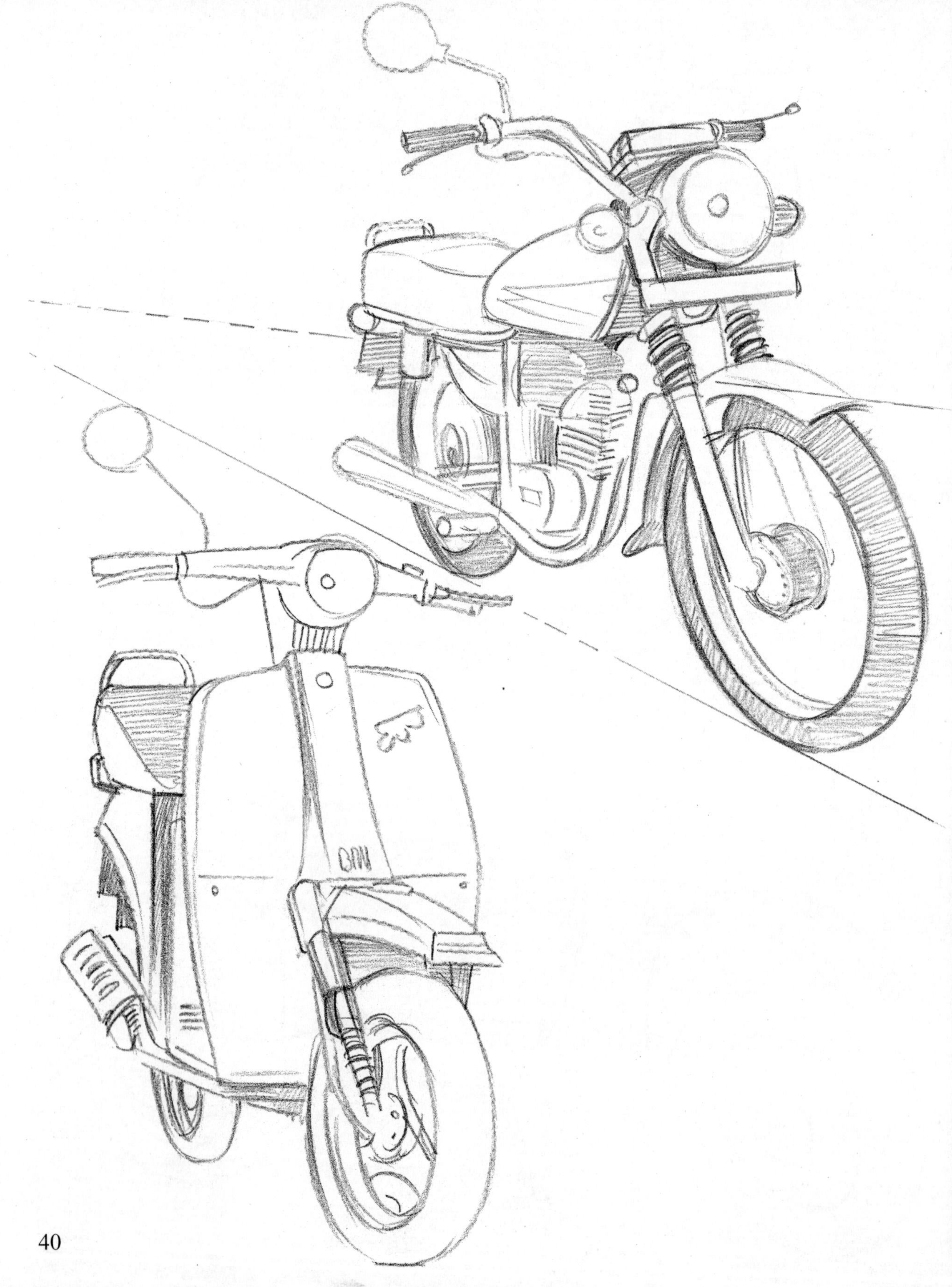

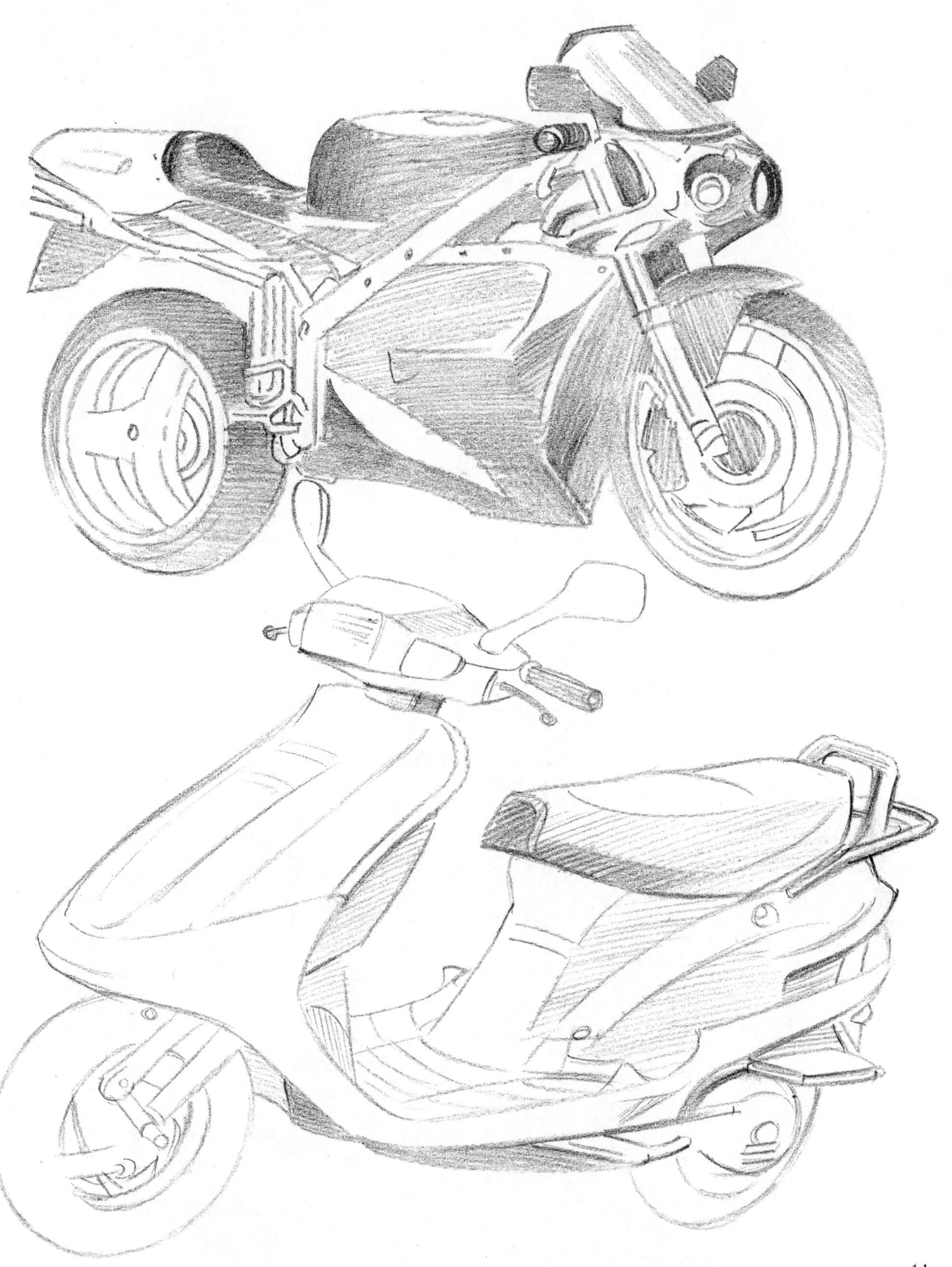

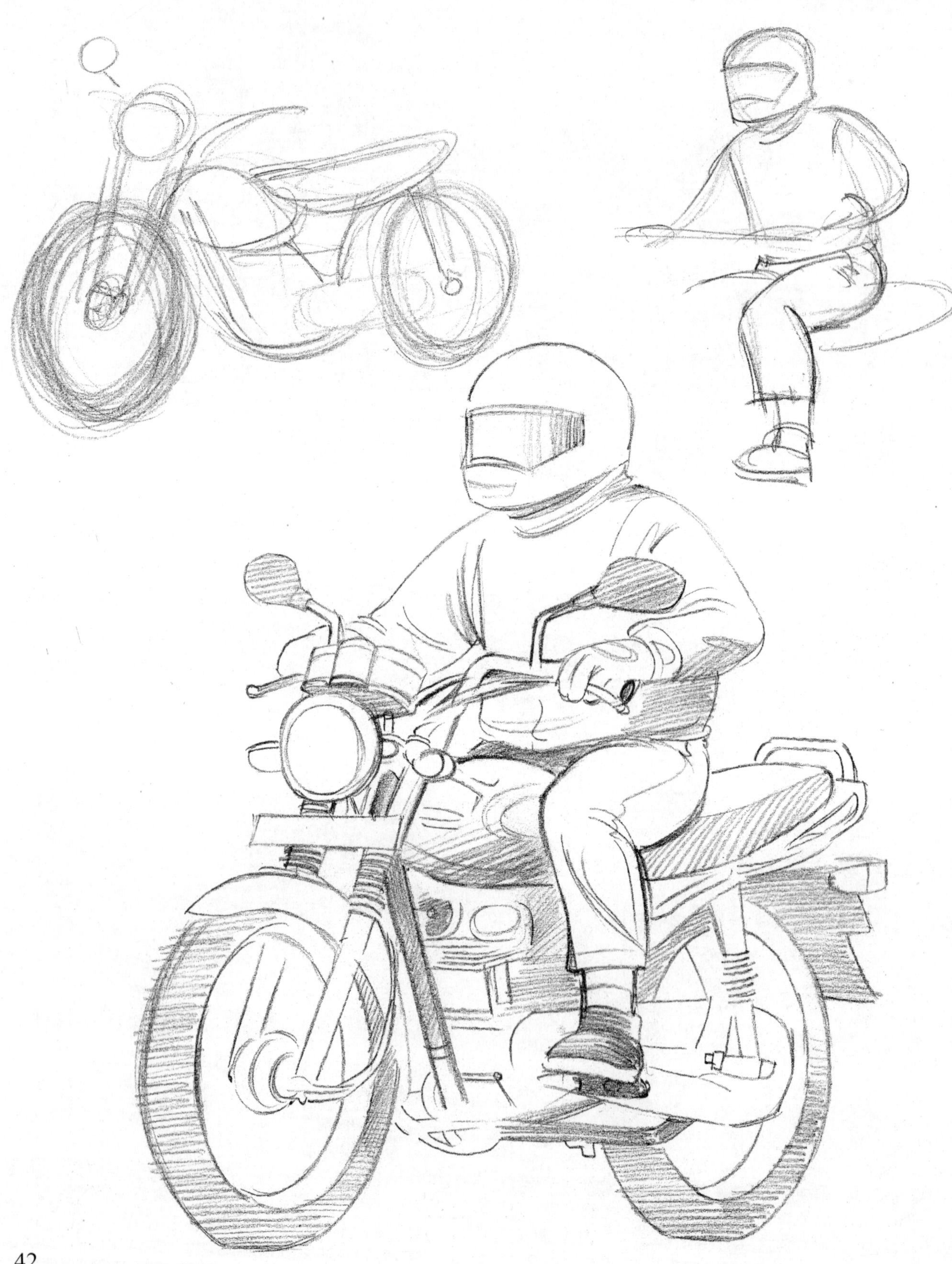

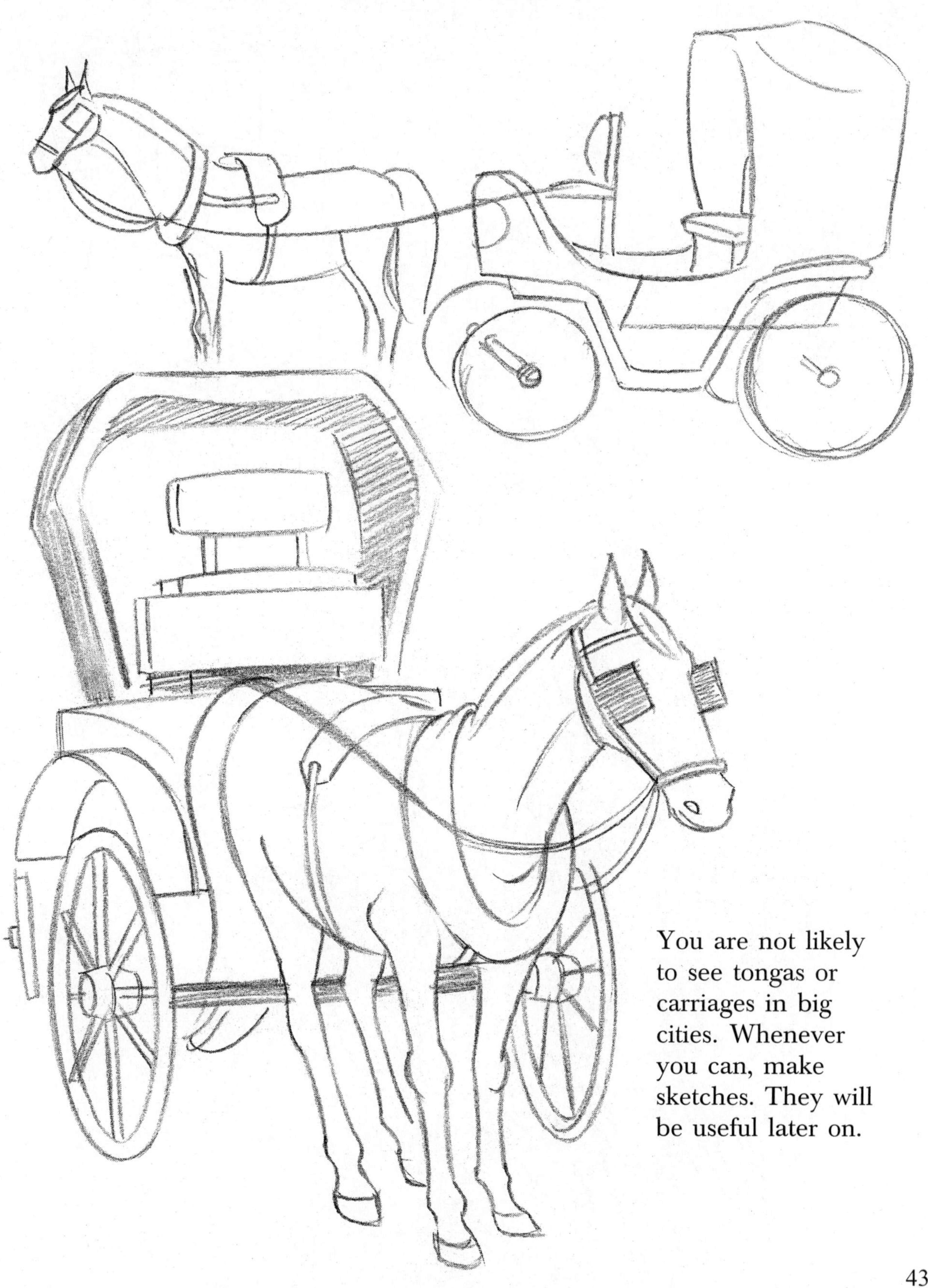

You are not likely to see tongas or carriages in big cities. Whenever you can, make sketches. They will be useful later on.

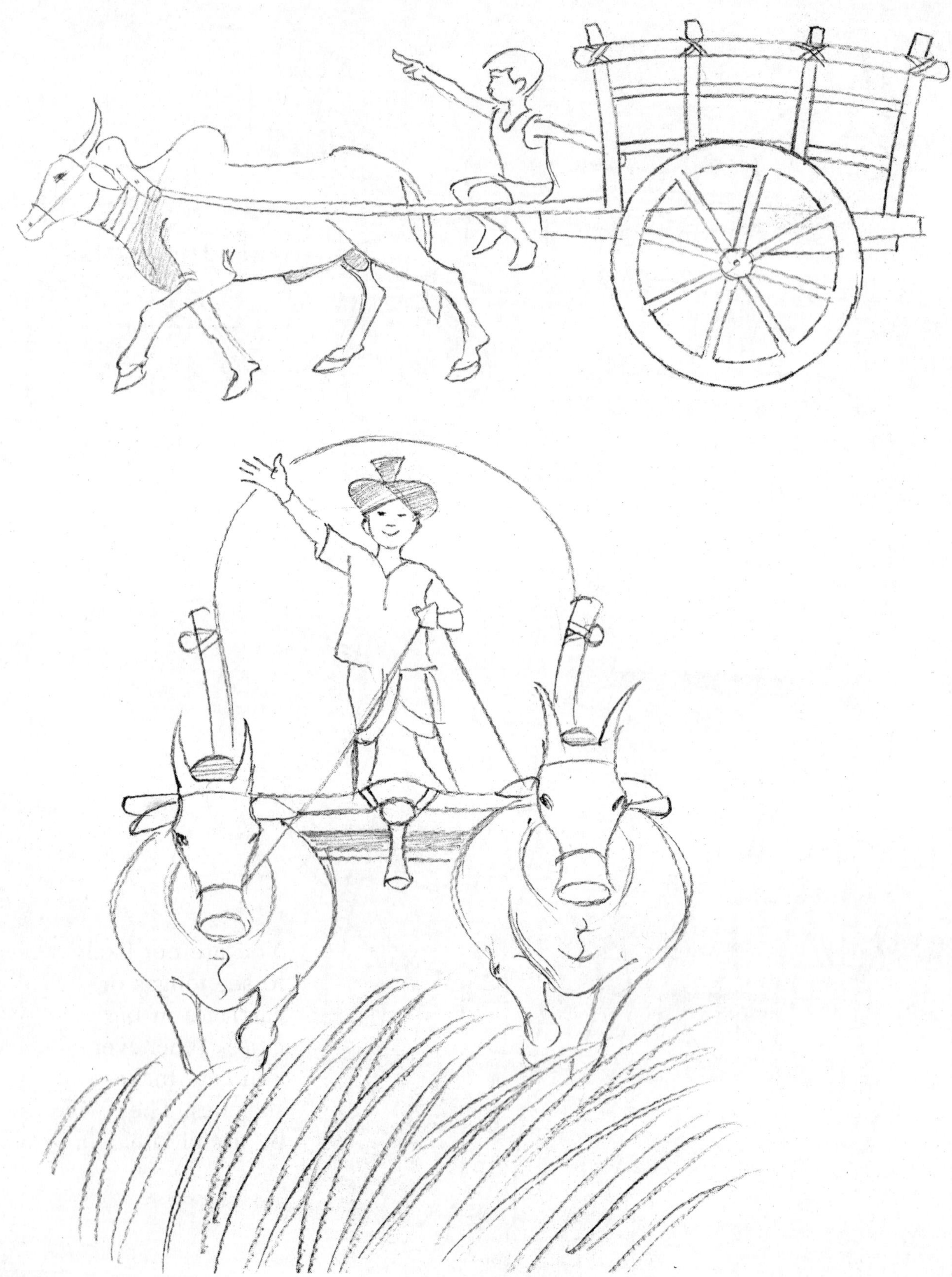

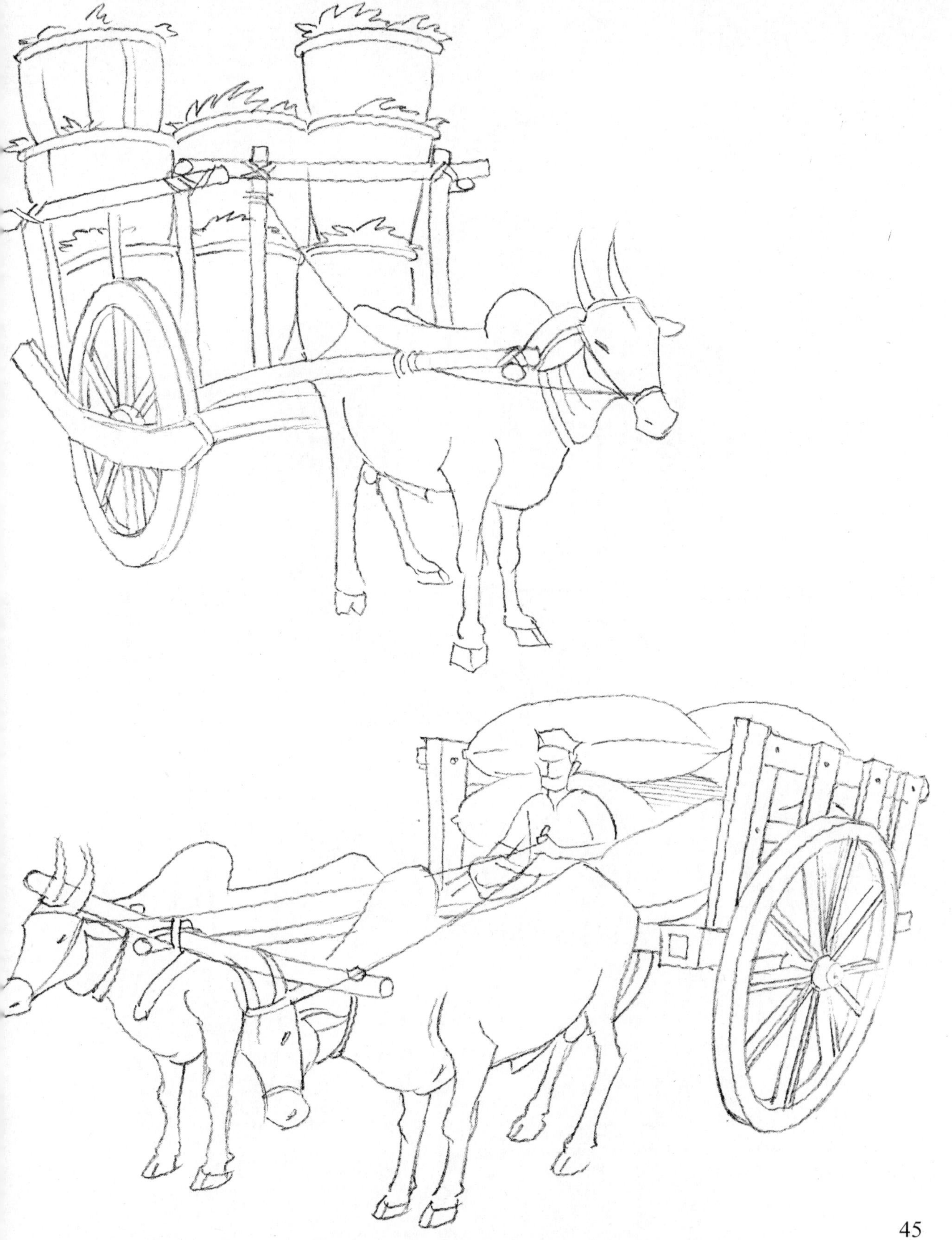

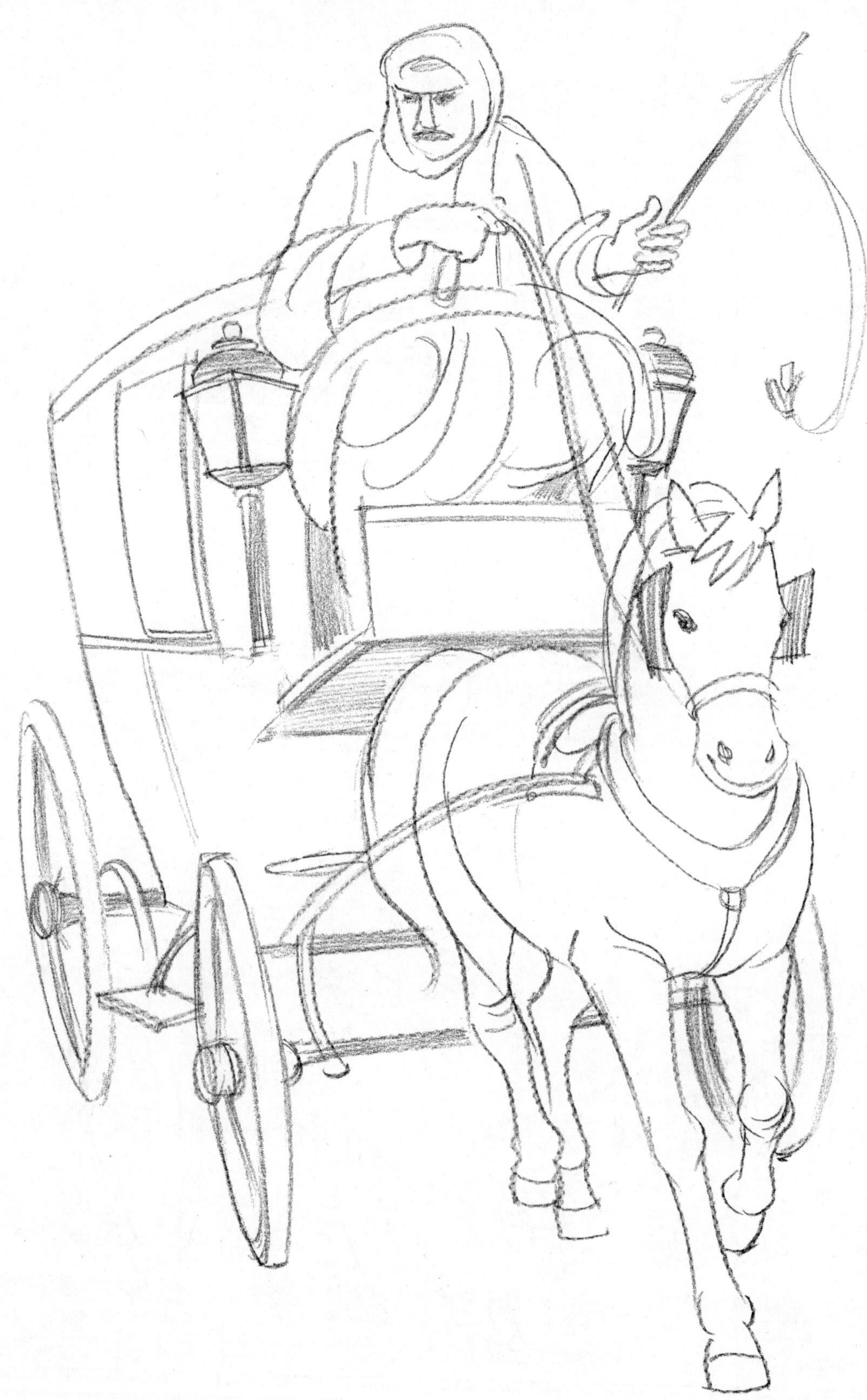

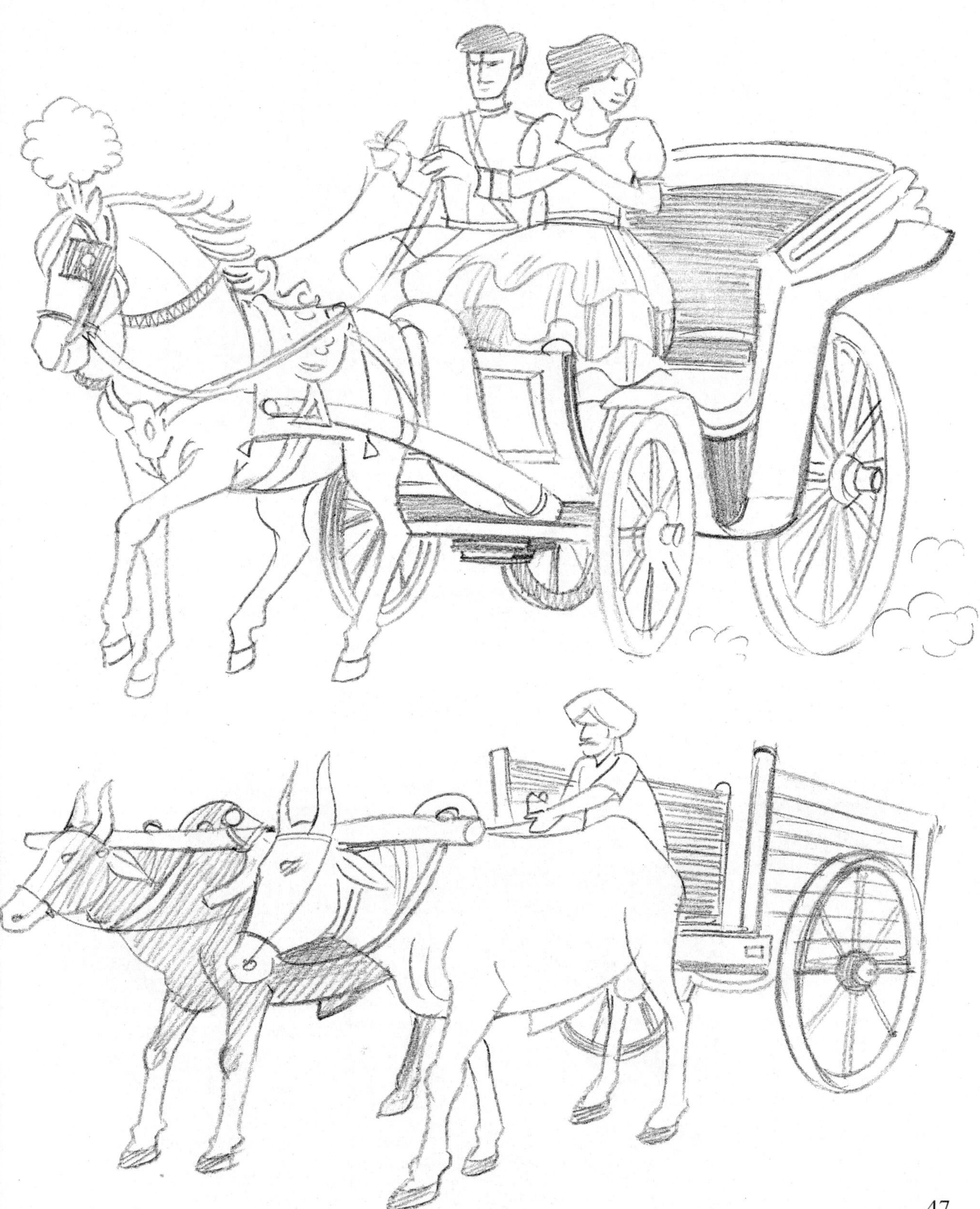

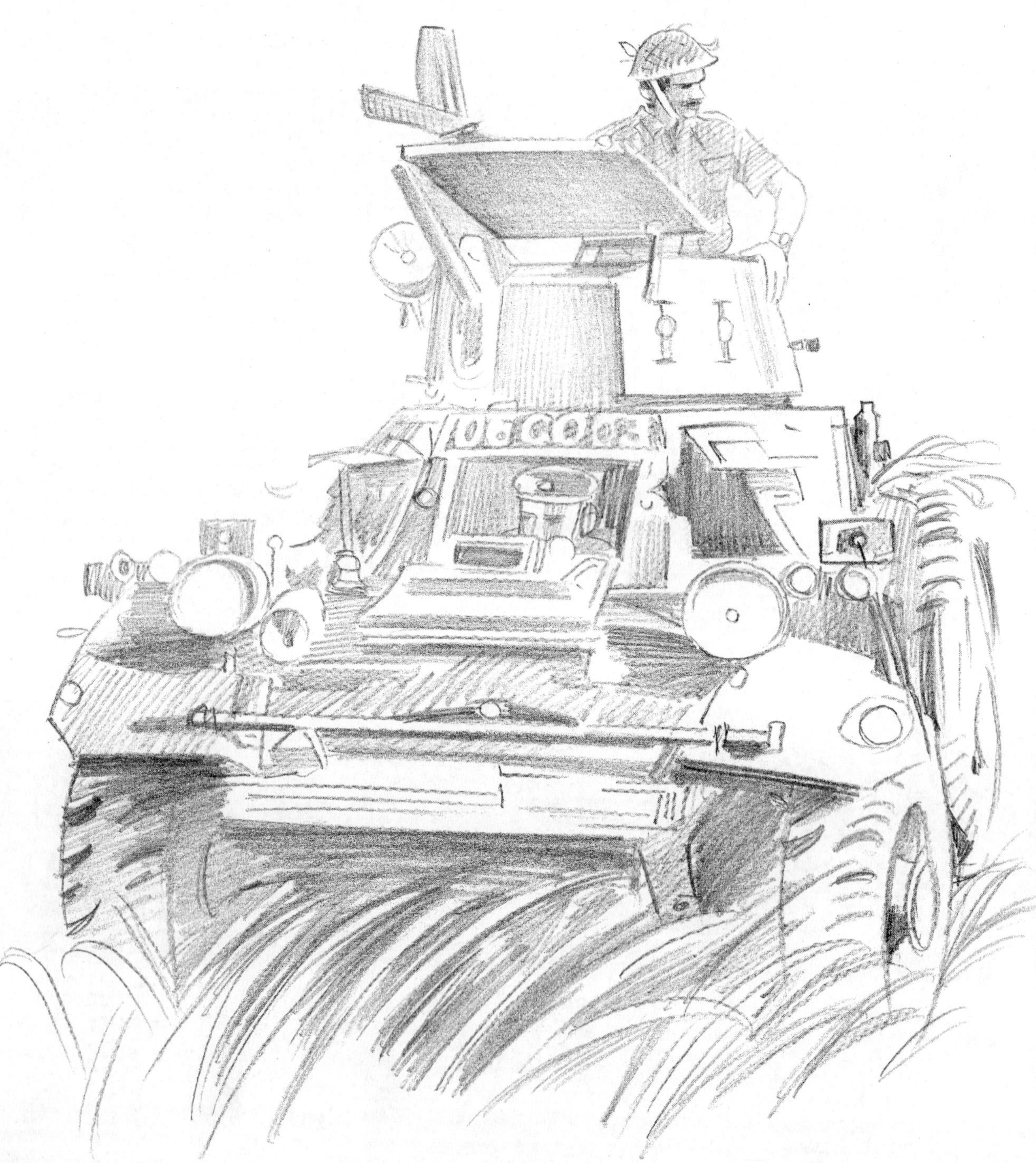